Pride
of the
Tyne

Coal staithes, c.1840.
(© Shipping Collection: Newcastle Libraries.)

Keith Durham & Máire West

First published in the United Kingdom in 2014 by Northern Heritage Publishing.
ISBN 9780954477738

Reprinted in paperback 2018
2nd edition published in the United Kingdom in 2018 by Northern Heritage Publishing.

Northern Heritage
Units 7&8 New Kennels, Blagdon Estate, Seaton Burn,
Newcastle upon Tyne NE13 6DB
Telephone: 01670 789 940
www.northern-heritage.co.uk

See our full online catalogue at www.northern-heritage.co.uk

Text copyright:
© 2014 Keith Durham and Máire West
Design and layout:
© 2014 Ian Scott Design

Printed in the UK by Martins the Printers (Berwick)

British Library Cataloguing in Publishing Data
A catalogue record for this book is available from the British Library.

ISBN: 9780995748576

The authors wish to thank the following people for their help:
Sarah Mulligan, Newcastle City Library Information Officer,
Graeme Peacock Photography, Lew Stringer, Geoff Newcomb and Ian Scott Design.

Front cover images:
Tyne Bridge under construction.
(Photo: © Newcastle Libaries.)

Anthony Gormley's Angel of the North
(Photo: © Graeme Peacock.)

Incandescent light bulb invented by Joseph Swan. (Photo: © Science Museum.)

Etching of Grey Street from *Reid's Handbook To Newcastle Upon Tyne*, published in 1863.

Back: Southbound express crossing King Edward VII Rail Bridge.   (Photo: © Gateshead Libraries.)

Contents

Tyneside is without doubt one of the most visited destinations in the country. So what is it that makes the region so special, not only to the Geordies who live there, but to visitors as well? Perhaps it's the region's world-class cultural venues, its legendary night-life, or its enviable tradition of sporting excellence? Or maybe it's Tyneside's rich diversity of architecture, its legacy of Victorian innovation and a heritage that stretches back to the Roman Emperor Hadrian and his renowned Wall? Or maybe it's the Geordies themselves that make Tyneside so special? Proud, energetic, resilient and warm-hearted, they work hard and play hard.

Tyneside's enduring popularity is, of course, due to a fusion of all these things - and much more besides. This book, which is broad in scope yet rich in detail, is an entertaining and informative look at the fascinating story of Tyneside from its early beginnings to the present day.

About the Authors

Keith Durham lives in Northumberland and is the author of *Discovering the North Pennines* (Northern Heritage), *The Border Reivers, Strongholds of the Border Reivers, Border Reiver 1513-1600, Viking Longship* (Osprey Publishing) and *Reivers - Anglo-Scottish Border Raiders from their origins to the end of the 16th Century* (Montlight Publishing).

Máire West moved to the North-East twenty-five years ago, via Galway, Dublin and Bonn. A specialist in Celtic Studies, she has contributed widely to books and periodicals on Celtic themes, specifically on Early Irish kingship and mythology. Her growing interest in the history of Newcastle and Northumberland has led to co-authorship with Ian Roberts of *Bellingham, North Tynedale and Redesdale* (Chalford) and she has edited a number of books including *Telling Tales out of School* (Northern Heritage) and *Brown Rigg School: Story of a Unique Institution* (The Heritage Centre at Bellingham).

PRIDE OF THE TYNE

Introduction

As most Geordies will agree, if you do have to leave Tyneside, whether journeying to far-flung destinations such as New York or Bangkok, or simply spending a day away at the York Races, one of the great joys of travelling is coming back home. No matter where you've been or how long you've been away, that first glimpse of Tyneside warms the heart and quickens the pulse.

Returning by air, panoramic views of the region unfold as your aircraft banks over the North-East coast. Golden beaches, rocky headlands, green fields and grey, sprawling conurbations slip by, and winding inland to the heart of Tyneside is the broad, glittering expanse of the River Tyne.

Many would argue that coming home by rail is an even richer experience, for on its final approach to Newcastle, the north-bound train crosses high above the River Tyne and passengers are treated to a stunning, bird's-eye view of the North-East's premier city. Looking out across elegant Victorian rooftops and the bustling quayside below, Gateshead's gossamer-like Millennium Bridge will certainly catch the eye; while to the north, the lofty spires of Newcastle's magnificent Cathedral of St Nicholas and the towering Norman Keep cannot fail to impress.

But dwarfing them all is the massive, soaring arc of the Tyne Bridge. Famous the world over and held in deep affection by Geordies both home and away, it's still the most potent symbol of Tyneside, and for those Geordies homeward-bound, the mere sight of that bridge is enough to brighten up their faces with big, happy, ear-to-ear smiles.

Tyneside is without doubt one of the most visited destinations in the country. So, just what is it that makes Tyneside so special, not only to Geordies but to visitors as well? Perhaps it's the legendary nightlife and the region's enviable tradition of sporting excellence, or the legacy of Victorian innovation and the unique collection of bridges that span the Tyne? Or maybe it's the world-class cultural venues, the city's rich diversity of architecture and a heritage that stretches back to the Roman Emperor Hadrian and his renowned Wall?

And let's not forget Newcastle Brown Ale, known better in the North-East as the 'Journey into Space'; our world-famous Geordie Sir Ridley Scott, director of *Gladiator*; the comedian Bobby Thompson, more affectionately known here as

'The Little Waster'; the musician, singer and song-writer known as Sting; that famous film *Get Carter*, shot in the North-East; that lovable Geordie cartoon character 'Biffa Bacon'; Bob Ferris and Terry Collier from the sixties TV sitcom *The Likely Lads*; world-famous footballer Jackie Milburn, known to all Geordies as 'Wor Jackie'. And of course, who could forget Newcastle United Football Club, famously tagged throughout the world as the 'Toon Army'?

Or maybe it's the Geordies themselves that make Tyneside so special? Proud, energetic, resilient and kind-hearted, they work hard and play hard. They are also blessed with a willingness to learn and master new skills and have been consistently successful in adapting to the monumental social and economic changes that have periodically swept across the region and disrupted their lives.

Tyneside, as we shall see, is a fusion of all of these things and much more besides. But in the beginning, and running like a gleaming, constant thread right down through our history to the present day, is the River Tyne.

From the air, Newcastle and Gateshead linked by the many bridges that cross the Tyne. (Photo: Graeme Peacock.)

1
THE RIVER TYNE

When contemplating the mighty Tyne of today, it is worthwhile remembering that when the Romans first began to harness the potential of this waterway, the river could be forded quite easily at a number of points at low tide. During the intervening centuries, the main channel and river mouth continued to suffer from heavy silting and both were cluttered with shoals and ever-shifting sandbanks, making navigation a tricky prospect even for skilled pilots.

In 1815, it was remarked that the river's banks were lined, not only with collieries, but factories, foundries and forges, glass houses, breweries and refineries, chemical works and shipbuilding yards. Yet in places the river was barely six feet deep. Even as late as 1846, when the Tyne was buzzing with a bewildering variety of shipping, it was reported that on one occasion the tide was so low that three river pilots were able to wade across the bar from the north side to the south! To make matters worse, prior to 1854 there were no piers at the river mouth and ships entering the Tyne were frequently blown off course and wrecked on the ominously named Black Middens Rocks, often with heavy loss of life.

By 1850, the Tyne Improvement Commissioners had taken over responsibility

Break in Tynemouth Pier in February 1901. The pier was rebuilt without a curve and was completed in 1909. (© Shipping Collection: Newcastle Libraries.)

for the river from Newcastle Corporation and, in order to realise the full potential of the waterway, they began a programme of straightening the riverbanks and dredging and deepening the river. By 1895, vast improvements were apparent. The long, protecting arms of the North and South Piers now sheltered the river mouth and even at low tide vessels could safely navigate as far upstream as Newcastle's Quayside without fear of running aground.

To guide ships across the bar, beacons were erected near the river mouth and positioned in such a way that navigators were able to plot a safe passage by lining up the two beacon lights when entering the Tyne. The two most prominent examples of these, built by John Stokoe circa 1808, are the white towers named High Light and Low Light, which replaced the High and Low Lights of 1727, and still dominate the North Shields Fish Quay to this day.

As a result of the improvements made by the Commissioners, larger ships could come and go, and during the industrial revolution the Tyne became a lucrative highway to the markets of the world. By the end of the nineteenth century, Tyneside had rapidly expanded to become Britain's largest exporter of coal and the most important centre of shipbuilding and armaments' manufacture in the world, bringing to the region a degree of economic wealth and prosperity which remains unsurpassed to this day.

Nowadays, attractive riverside housing complexes, marinas, business parks, and retail outlet centres are gradually replacing the heavy industry that once thrived along the banks of the Tyne, bringing life back to this great river and in the process, creating a vibrant, new lifestyle for the twenty-first century.

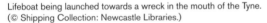

Lifeboat being launched towards a wreck in the mouth of the Tyne.
(© Shipping Collection: Newcastle Libraries.)

2
TYNEMOUTH

Perched high on the northern headland that overlooks the river mouth, stands the imposing fourteenth-century gatehouse of Tynemouth Castle, and within the castle grounds lie the picturesque ruins of Tynemouth Priory. During the Dark Ages, Viking longships prowled this rocky coastline and in AD 865, marauding Danes sacked the original monastery. The priory was refounded in the eleventh century by the Benedictine monks of Durham and was the temporary burial-place of the Scottish king, Malcolm Canmore, who was killed in battle at Alnwick in 1093. His body was later exhumed and re-buried at Dunfermline Abbey, alongside other Scottish kings and queens, by order of Alexander the First of Scotland.

As early as 1095, there was a castle consisting of earthen ramparts and a wooden stockade standing on the same site as the priory. In 1296, King Edward I, the 'Hammer of the Scots', gave orders that the priory should be properly fortified with walls of stone, and still later in 1390, a gatehouse and barbican were added to the landward side of the castle. Guarding the approach to the river, Tynemouth Castle saw continuous service throughout the Middle Ages and even at the time of the English Civil War, it was described as being well-fortified, with very good guns, but its fair church had fallen into decay.

In the days before foreign holidays were as accessible as they are now, Tynemouth's long, golden sands and rocky coves made the town a hugely popular seaside resort. Rows of substantial Victorian terraced houses, both on the seafront and in the town's side streets, offered a wide variety of guesthouse accommodation and many Tyneside families traditionally spent their summer holidays there.

The summers are quieter now, but those same beaches still attract their share of visitors, and more recently windsurfers, who really appreciate the resort's long, rolling breakers. In common with much of Tyneside, the town is linked to the Metro, Tyne and Wear's rapid transit system and at weekends, its Victorian railway station hosts a vibrant antiques, collectables, bric-a-brac and general market, one of the busiest in the North-East.

To the west of the castle, in splendid isolation, stands an elegant monument to one of Tyneside's great unsung heroes, Admiral Lord Collingwood. Born in 1748 into a family in reduced circumstances living at the Side in Newcastle-upon-

Tyne, Cuthbert Collingwood left the Royal Grammar School at the age of twelve and went to sea as a volunteer on board the frigate HMS *Shannon*, under the command of his cousin Captain (later Admiral) Richard Braithwaite, who took charge of his nautical education in the Royal Navy.

In a long and distinguished career, Collingwood was to see frequent active service against the Spanish and the French, but his finest hour undoubtedly came at the Battle of Trafalgar on 21 October 1805. After his close friend Horatio Nelson was killed early in this engagement, Collingwood in his flagship *Royal Sovereign*, took command of the British fleet, and through his inspired leadership the Royal Navy was able to fulfil Nelson's battle plan and inflict a devastating defeat on the combined French and Spanish fleets. In grateful recognition of his loyal services, Collingwood was promoted to Vice-Admiral of the Red and raised to the peerage as Baron Collingwood of Caldburne and Hethpool in the County of Northumberland. He also received the thanks of both Houses of Parliament and was awarded a pension of £2000 per annum.

When not at sea, he usually resided at his country retreat called Collingwood House, his beloved home in Morpeth, some fifteen miles north of Newcastle. He enjoyed taking long walks in the countryside with his dog Bounce and always took handfuls of acorns in his pockets. As he walked, he would press an acorn into the soil whenever he saw a good place to grow an oak tree. It is said that he did this to ensure that England's Navy would never be short of the strong oak with which to build her fighting ships.

In 1805, he was appointed to the Commander-in-Chief Mediterranean Fleet, taking part in many political and diplomatic transactions, and was greatly admired for his tact and good judgement. In subsequent years, his earnest requests to be relieved of his command so that he might return home, all fell on deaf ears on the grounds that the country could not dispense with the services of such an experienced commander. However, during 1809, Admiral Lord Collingwood's health began seriously to decline and at last he was granted permission by the Admiralty to return home. But sadly, he was never to see his native shores again and died on board the *Ville de Paris*, off Port Mahon, as he sailed for England on 7 March 1810. His body was returned to England and buried with full honours. He was laid to rest beside his great friend Nelson in the crypt of St Paul's Cathedral in London.

Flanked by four cannon from his beloved *Royal Sovereign*, Admiral Lord Collingswood's towering statue gazes out for evermore across Tyne's river mouth to the open seas beyond, a fine memorial to a local hero who seems forever destined to be overshadowed by his famous and more flamboyant friend.

Nearby stands The Brigade Watch House, headquarters of the Tynemouth Volunteer Life Brigade (TVLB), a voluntary, shore-based, coastal rescue service.

The Brigade Watch House, headquarters of The Tynemouth Volunteer Life Brigade (TVLB). (Photo: Graeme Peacock.)

Founded in 1864, in answer to an appeal by John Morrison who, together with many other helpless spectators, witnessed the shipwreck of two vessels, the schooner *Friendship* and the passenger steamer *Stanley*, caught in a fierce, south-easterly gale at sea and driven ashore on to the infamous Black Middens Rocks at the mouth of the River Tyne. There and then he vowed to do something about it.

At that time, the Coastguard at Tynemouth consisted of four men only, two of whom were pensioners. Despite their best efforts to use the breeches buoy to rescue those on the vessels, the lines became hopelessly entangled and the lifeboats which joined the rescue effort were also unsuccessful. By dawn the next morning, thirty-two people had died in this maritime disaster. It was apparent to John Morrison that had there been a body of men trained and disciplined to assist the Coastguard, many of those who perished could have been saved. The TVLB was founded at a public meeting in North Shields Town Hall on 5 December 1864 and was the first organisation of its kind in Britain working alongside the Lifeboat Association. Its legacy to present-day Tynesiders, the Brigade Watch House Museum, open to visitors six days a week, hosts a display of artefacts, pictures, nautical memorabilia and relics from old shipwrecks, chronicling the history of lifesaving on our coastline since 1864.

Fishing boats at Low Light, North Shields Fish Quay, c.1900. (© Shipping Collection: Newcastle Libraries.)

3

NORTH SHIELDS

An enjoyable way to explore both sides of the river and in the process, get a unique perspective of the river mouth, is to take a trip across the Tyne on one of the two foot-passenger ferries, *Pride of the Tyne* and *Spirit of the Tyne*. The former was built by the old Swan Hunter Company and launched in 1993, and the latter by VT Halmatic in Portchester and launched in 2007. These ferries run on a regular basis between North Shields and South Shields. Both towns have a long association with the fishing industry, the name 'shields' being derived from Medieval English *schele*, meaning 'a temporary shed or hut used by early settlers'.

The town we know today as North Shields was originally a small settlement founded in the thirteenth century by Prior Germanus as a fishing port for the priory at Tynemouth, to provide fish for his monks and to victual ships anchored nearby. Some rudimentary houses or 'shiels', as well as some wooden quays, were erected at the mouth of the Pow Burn where it enters the Tyne for this purpose. The quays were also used by the prior to ship coal from the priory pits at Tynemouth. Due to the demand for fish the settlement prospered and by the beginning of the sixteenth century, a lucrative salt trade had also developed, more permanent quays had been built and breweries and bakehouses flourished.

At the beginning of the eighteenth century, North Shields was a large, well-built and popular seaport situated at the very confluence of the River Tyne with the sea, with a thriving salt trade which was invaluable for curing fish. Although the trade in salt petered out after a while, the demand for fish remained undiminished and an extensive herring-fishery industry developed, which used North Shields as a base.

The North Shields Fish Quay, which was opened in 1870, became a magnet for fishing fleets not only from the North-East, but from all over the northern hemisphere. Fish processing sheds were erected and in order to cope with the influx of boats, the Quay was repeatedly extended. In those days of the great herring fleets at the turn of the twentieth century, faded photographs from that period show North Shields Fish Quay packed to capacity with ships and boats of all shapes and sizes. Beneath a maze of masts, fishermen tend their herring drifters and repair nets and, on the quayside, warehouses and chandlers' shops overflowed with the paraphernalia of the fishing industry. In 1877, a certain North Shields tug-owner named William Purdy fitted trawl gear to the paddle-tug *Messenger*, thus pioneering the use of steam-trawling on the River Tyne. By 1909, ships were landing in excess of 20,000 tons of herring a year.

In those days too, the river's banks resounded to the clang of the riveter's hammer and the shipyards of Tyneside boomed. On the river, old photographs show paddleboats and colliers billowing clouds of sooty smoke, steaming busily up and down the Tyne. Small boats weave perilously close to tall, sedate liners and their accompanying tugs, and further upriver the silhouettes of giant cranes and huge warships darken the skyline. Such scenes, however, are now a thing of the past.

An intrinsic part of the history of North Shields are the 'Wooden Dollies'. In 1814, the female figurehead of a collier brig was placed at the entrance to Custom House Quay on Liddell Street, and stood there until 1850 when unfortunately, it was vandalised. Successive Dollies were placed on the same spot and defaced by fishermen as a source of good luck. Pieces of wood were shaved off the Dollies and taken by these seafarers as good luck charms for their voyages. In 1992, the sixth 'Wooden Dolly' was put in place at the entrance to Custom House quay and can still be seen there, right next door to the Prince of Wales public house.

Although Tyneside's fishing industry is a mere shadow of its former self, the maritime roots go deep nonetheless. Despite diminishing catches and what they perceive as flawed legislation formulated by people who do not understand the sea, a handful of fishermen still sail out frequently from North Shields to wrest a living from the grey, capricious North Sea.

Nowadays, the North Shields Fish Quay is a popular destination for locals and tourists alike, and people are still drawn to the bustle of activity when the boats come in and the fishermen unload their catch. The Fish Quay is also home to some of the best fish-and-chip shops in the region and it is pleasant indeed to stroll along the quayside on a summer's evening, watching the world drift by and enjoying a delicious 'fish supper' right next to the River Tyne. And if you're not actually a real Geordie, well . . . at least you can pretend!

Further upriver, near the Swan Hunter shipyard at Wallsend, stands the excavated remains of the Roman fort of Segedunum. The first of seventeen forts built along Hadrian's Wall, Segedunum, which may mean 'strong fort' in Romano-British, was strategically sited on a bend of the river, giving lookouts a clear view both up and downstream. The fort, which was an important military base, covered a little over four acres and could house a garrison of up to six hundred soldiers, both cavalry and infantry.

Marking the beginning and end of the new 84-mile, long-distance Hadrian's Wall Path National Trail, Segedunum is the most thoroughly excavated fort on the Wall. The site can be viewed from a unique, 35-metre high observation tower and the complete layout of a Roman fort can be seen clearly from this vantage point. Segedunum is also home to a reconstructed Roman military bath-house, which can be heated by a replica of the original, underfloor heating system. In the award-winning museum, a display of articles found on the site and a variety of models and reconstructions give visitors a vivid insight into what life must have been like on this frontier of the Roman Empire. Part of the original Wall can also be seen and alongside it, an impressive reconstructed section shows how the Wall may have looked 1,800 years ago.

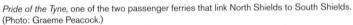

Pride of the Tyne, one of the two passenger ferries that link North Shields to South Shields. (Photo: Graeme Peacock.)

4
SOUTH SHIELDS

On the south side of the river mouth stands South Shields. The town was founded in 1245 and developed as a fishing port. As with North Shields, the name developed from the Medieval English *schele*, meaning 'a temporary shed or hut used by early settlers'. Salt-panning expanded as an industry here in the fifteenth century.

Always an industrious area, the town was never more so than in the nineteenth century, when coal mining, alkaline production and glass making led to a boom in expansion. The population increased from 12,000 in 1801 to 75,000 in the 1860s. These industries created a great deal of regional wealth. However, the rapid growth in population brought its own problems, including a number of outbreaks of cholera and the building of the now listed Cleadon Water Tower and Pumping Station, opened in 1860 to improve sanitation.

The town has strong links with the sea and its world-famous Marine School, founded in 1861 as South Shields Marine College and now a part of South Tyneside College, has a worldwide reputation second to none for outstanding maritime training. Since its foundation, students have come from every corner of the globe to be instructed in the arts of navigation and seamanship, marine and electrical engineering, communications and other nautical sciences.

Seafarers have another good reason to be eternally thankful for the town's maritime heritage. In 1789, the tragic loss of a Newcastle ship named *Adventure*, wrecked in rough seas off the mouth of the Tyne only 275 metres from the shore and its crew swept out to drown at sea, proved to be a timely catalyst for the commissioning of designs for a 'lifeboat'. A public meeting was held and money raised for the best lifeboat design. The prize was divided between William Woodhave, a parish clerk, and Henry Greathead, a boat-builder from South Shields, both of whom submitted models of a self-righting lifeboat. The world's first self-righting lifeboat, called *Original*, incorporating elements of both their designs, was launched in 1790. She served for forty years and saved hundreds of lives from the fierce North Sea. A fitting memorial to both these men can be seen on the town's aptly named Ocean Road and on display nearby is *Tyne*, the second lifeboat to be built at South Shields. Launched in 1833 and serving for over 60 years, she saved over one thousand lives before being honourably retired in 1894.

In the 1850s, the shipbuilding industry around South Shields was rapidly

Aerial view of Tyne Dock, Jarrow in 1949. (© Shipping Collection: Newcastle Libraries.)

expanding and in 1859, Tyne Dock was opened at Jarrow Slake, a large area of tidal mud-flats. In the early 1880s, John Redhead moved upriver to the western part of South Shields, next to Tyne Dock, because his shipyard at Lawe had become too small for his shipbuilding operation which by then was employing well over a thousand men. By the year 1900, South Shields was at the forefront of Britain's shipbuilding industry, turning out twenty vessels a year. In addition, thriving support industries along the river bank fitted out these ships, supplying chains, anchors, ropes and timber and the town of South Shields prospered accordingly.

Two fine seafront areas, North and South Marine Parks, were opened in the 1890s, and a select array of shops also sprang up, offering goods from across the world to those who could afford them. The town's increasing wealth was also reflected in the building of its stately Town Hall and impressive Customs House. The latter now houses a popular art gallery, theatre and cinema. Like Tynemouth, South Shields enjoyed a long period when its parks, seafront and beaches made it a popular holiday destination, but sadly, when the shipbuilding and coal industries shrank, so too did much of the town's Victorian air of prosperity.

Nowadays, hi-technology businesses have replaced the town's dependence on heavy industry to a large degree and South Shields has once again become a bustling seaside town with a vibrant night-life and a wide selection of restaurants, serving up some of the finest ethnic cuisine in the region. The town also has some splendid, traditional Tyneside pubs, each with its own unique character. Amongst these are The Steamboat, situated down by the ferry landing, and The Harbour Lights and The Beacon situated on Lawe Top, which offer good food, fine ales and stunning views across the river mouth.

Mural by Bob Olley on the wall of The Beacon, South Shields. (Photo: Keith Durham.)

This area is also the renowned 'Catherine Cookson Country' and admirers of that prolific and much loved author make pilgrimages here from all over the world to explore the area where she was born and spent her formative years. South Shields Museum and Art Gallery houses a Catherine Cookson Gallery, where there is a reconstruction of the façade of Number 10 William Black Street and its kitchen where the author spent her early years, Cissie Affleck's shop, and an exhibition where visitors can see how the working classes of South Tyneside lived in the early part of the twentieth century.

Not far from the town centre, standing on the Lawe Top overlooking the River Tyne and guarding the seaward entrance to what was once Rome's most northerly outpost, are the remains of the Roman fort of Arbeia. Founded around AD 120, it became the maritime supply fort for the other forts along Hadrian's Wall and contains the only permanent stone-built granaries as yet found in Britain.

Working alongside the soldiers stationed at Arbeia were civilians from every corner of the Roman Empire. Besides acting as river pilots, their many tasks included unloading supplies from the larger ships and ferrying them further upstream in smaller boats. Appropriately enough, one possible meaning for Arbeia is 'fort of the Arab troops', referring to the fact that at one time part of it garrison was a squadron of Mesopotamian boatmen from the Tigris, now modern-day Iraq. A squadron of Spanish cavalry, the First Asturians, was also stationed there.

Today, standing alongside the excavated remains of the fort are full-scale reconstructions

The bronze figures 'Conversation Piece', Little Haven Beach, South Shields were created by Juan Muñoz. Behind stands Herd Groyne lighthouse and across the river can be seen Tynemouth Priory and Brigade Watch House. (Photo: Graeme Peacock.)

13

of the barrack block and the spacious commanding officer's house, dating from around AD 300. Perhaps most impressive of all, however, is the reconstruction of the fortified West Gate. Standing three storeys high, the tower on this serves as a museum detailing the life of a Roman soldier, while from its ramparts new `zlegions of visitors can enjoy sweeping views of the River Tyne.

Further upstream, near the town of Jarrow, lies Jarrow Hall – Anglo-Saxon Farm, Village and Bede Museum (formerly named Bede's World). The Venerable Bede (AD 672/3 – 735) was a monk, ordained priest, world-famous theologian and scholar, who lived and worked at the monasteries of Jarrow and Wearmouth. During the Golden Age of Northumbria, which dated from the beginning of the seventh to the early ninth centuries, Bede stood out as Europe's greatest scholar and historian. He wrote about forty books, mainly dealing with theology and history, including commentaries on the Bible, observations on nature, music and poetry. His most famous work, a key source for the understanding of early British history, is entitled *Historia Ecclesiastica Gentis Anglorum* ('the Ecclesiastical History of the English People'), which he completed in AD 731.

Attractions here include a fascinating museum with exhibitions exploring Bede's life and work, the life of a monk and the medieval kingdom of Northumbria. Among the reconstructed buildings are a monk's cell, a *Grubenhaus* or 'sunken building' used for cold storage, a fully working, reconstructed Anglo-Saxon farm, stocked with rare animal breeds and the renovated, eighteenth-century Jarrow Hall House.

Nearby stands the historic St Paul's Monastery, which retains intact in its oldest section the original, seventh-century stained-glass window of aqua, yellow, green and brown. This is extremely important as it is the earliest example of coloured glass in Britain which can still be seen *in situ*. There are many other stone carvings inside the church which date from the time of Bede, and the ruined walls of the medieval monastery can still clearly be traced on the grounds outside.

Bede Museum, Jarrow. (Photo: Graeme Peacock.)

Newcastle-upon-Tyne, 1745 by Nathanial Buck. (© Newcastle Libraries.)

5

NEWCASTLE-UPON-TYNE

The beginning

When the Emperor Hadrian ordered the construction of the world-famous Wall in AD 122 that still bears his name, Roman engineers built the first bridge across a narrow stretch of the River Tyne, more or less where the Swing Bridge stands today. Built of timber and raised on stone piers, the bridge was named Pons Aelius in honour of Hadrian, whose full name was Publius Aelius Hadrianus, his family name being Aelius.

In order to defend the crossing, a fort of the same name was built upon the steep-sided headland that dominated the northern end of the bridge. In time, a thriving settlement, or *vicus*, grew up around the fort, which would form the nucleus of modern-day Newcastle-upon-Tyne. Before Hadrian's Wall was extended to Segedunum (at modern-day Wallsend), Pons Aelius marked the eastern terminus of the 117-kilometre (73-mile) long Wall and was garrisoned by the First Cohort of Cornovii, an infantry unit five hundred strong. The Wall was constructed primarily to prevent unwanted immigration and incursion of the Pictish tribes from the north, whom the Romans considered uncivilised.

Various artefacts from the period of Roman occupation, both military and civilian, have been discovered in and around the area where the Castle Keep now stands. When the Romans left Britain in the early fifth century, this settlement fell into ruins and the area then became part of the powerful Anglo-Saxon Kingdom of Northumbria. Anglo-Saxon monks may have settled there for a while because the area was known in Anglo-Saxon times as Monkchester, but after a series of conflicts with the Danes and the Normans, Monkchester was all but destroyed.

The medieval town

After the Norman Conquest in 1066, the north of England remained a turbulent and rebellious area for many years. Even after William conquered the region in 1071, the inhabitants of the region remained unsubdued. In the spring of 1080, they rebelled against the rule of Walcher, Earl of Northumbria and William despatched his half-brother, Odo of Bayeux, to deal with the rebellion and teach them a lesson by devastating the whole region. In the autumn of 1080, William's eldest son, Robert Curthose, Duke of Normandy, was sent to lead a military campaign against the Scots and on his return to England, he built a wooden fortress from which to pacify the area and enforce Norman rule. Utilising the same strategic position that the Romans had chosen for their fort, this new castle was a typical motte-and-bailey construction, consisting of a wooden tower on top of an earthen mound or motte, surrounded by a moat and wooden stockade or bailey. Part of the deep ditch still runs between the railway bridge and the Black Gate and can be seen today. It was this new castle structure that actually gave Newcastle its name.

This wooden castle served its purpose until 1168, when its replacement was begun with a much stronger construction in stone, on the orders of Henry II. The new fortification, which took ten years to complete, consisted of an imposing keep, a gatehouse and a substantial curtain wall, the enclosed area becoming known as the Castle Garth. In the thirteenth century, a great hall was added and, in order to reinforce the western side of the castle which is the only area in the complex without strong natural protection, the original gatehouse was replaced by a much grander structure. Built between 1247 and 1250, the new structure formed an additional barbican in front of the north gate of the castle. It consisted of two towers and a passage running between them, with a vaulted guardroom on either side. There was a drawbridge at the front which faced west and another at the rear. There was also a portcullis which could be raised and lowered to seal the entrance passage. In later years, this new gatehouse became known as the Black Gate.

In the thirteenth century, England's most obvious foes were the Scots, whose attacks invariably came from the north. As a consequence, most Northumbrian castles were defensively situated on the south banks of the region's rivers. It is interesting, therefore, to note that the fortifications at Newcastle were positioned

on the north bank of the Tyne, in order to protect the vital bridgehead and allow English kings to use the castle as a power base for their frequent incursions into Scotland.

The Town Wall, begun in 1265, took almost one hundred years to complete. Built in a protective loop around the town, the wall also extended along the riverbank. Massively strong, it stood up to 7.6 metres (25 feet) high, was at least 2 metres (6.5 feet) thick and incorporated along its three-kilometre (two-mile) length six major gates (Close Gate, West Gate, New Gate, Pilgrim Gate, Pandon Gate and Sand Gate), seventeen towers, as well as several smaller turrets and postern gates. In 1540, it was observed by the English poet, John Leyland, that the *'strength and magnificens of the waulling of this town far passeth al the waulles of the cities of England, and most of the townes of Europe'.*

Throughout the duration of the Border Wars, which began in the late thirteenth century and lasted some three hundred years, the castle was safely enclosed within the town's walls and its increasing use as little more than a supply base eventually led to the curtain wall and the Castle Keep falling into decay. In 1644, the castle was briefly refortified and saw action during the English Civil War.

In later years, the Keep and the Black Gate gradually fell into even further decay until in the nineteenth century, they were both restored to their present, somewhat altered appearance. Unfortunately, in the mid-nineteenth century, amidst a surge of Victorian enterprise, the curtain wall between the Keep and the Black Gate was completely demolished in order to make way for a railway viaduct. Unsurprisingly, some of the Keep's stark grandeur has suffered as a result, as commuter trains clatter past mere yards from its once forbidding walls. Fortunately, quite a few sections of the town's wall, along with some of its towers, have survived the worst purges of subsequent generations. One of the best-preserved stretches of the wall stands near Bath Lane and Stowell Street, where

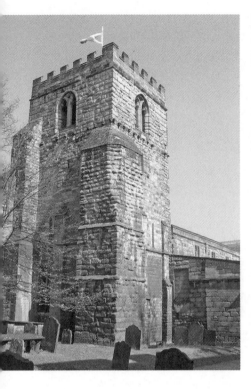

The present Parish Church of St Andrew was begun in the twelfth century. It is traditionally recognised as the oldest church in Newcastle and there was possibly an earlier church on this site dating from Saxon times. (Photo: Ian Scott.)

its rugged tower and blackened stones still give some idea of the sheer scale of Newcastle town's medieval fortifications.

Within its stout belt of protective walls, the medieval town began to grow quite rapidly and soon boasted a number of friaries and churches, the finest of which was undoubtedly the Church of St Nicholas, patron saint of sailors and boats. Built of sandstone and dating mainly from the thirteenth and fourteenth centuries, the interior of the church is endowed with a wealth of architectural and historic details. A most unusual lantern spire, constructed in 1448, crowns the tower of this magnificent church. For hundreds of years this was a main navigation point for ships using the River Tyne and at one time a light was kept burning in the tower to aid mariners on their course to port. At its base the tower measures 11.2 metres by 11 metres and it is approximately 60 metres from the base to the top of the steeple. St Nicholas's Church became a cathedral in 1882, when the Diocese of Newcastle was created by Queen Victoria. A much admired and distinctive landmark, the soaring spires of the Cathedral Church of St Nicholas have dominated Newcastle's skyline for centuries.

Nearby, on the corner of present-day Grainger Street and Westgate Road, stands the more modest parish church of St John. Built in the thirteenth century, the chancel, now the Lady Chapel, contains a window which includes fragments of medieval glass with the earliest known representation of Newcastle's armorial bearings – three white turrets on a red field. To the north, another church called St Andrew's, was established in the twelfth century beside the Newgate and is traditionally recognised as the oldest church in Newcastle. Much extended in later centuries, its sturdy tower still stands only a few yards from a looming section of the town wall.

During the early years of the thirteenth century, orders of friars began to establish themselves throughout England. Of the five friaries or monasteries built in Newcastle at this time, only Black Friars survives. After the dissolution of the monasteries in 1536, this Dominican monastery was sold to the town's rich merchants (also called burgesses) and subsequently leased to nine of Newcastle's craft guilds, to be used as their headquarters. Although most of the monastery has been long since demolished, the picturesque cloisters, lying between Forth Street and Stowell Street, now house a number of craft shops and a restaurant.

For quite some time, the area around the Castle remained the focal point of the town. Markets thrived in the vicinity of St Nicholas's Church and a street pattern began to emerge that we would recognise today. One of the earliest streets in Newcastle was the Side. Leading from St Nicholas's, this is a steep, narrow passage winding right down beneath the Black Gate to the banks of the River Tyne.

Medieval economic growth

On the medieval riverside, piers were erected to facilitate the loading of ships and in time, as parts of the riverbank were reclaimed, these piers were broadened, the spaces between them filled up with debris and a rudimentary quayside was formed. As a consequence, English coastal traders and foreign ships began to arrive in ever-increasing numbers with the passage of time, so that the town's merchants prospered and the port of Newcastle flourished. A succession of royal charters, legal privileges and restrictive trading practices allowed the town to create monopolies effectively, both in the market place and on the river.

Due to its control of the River Tyne, the revenues received from its various ports and the shipping that passed along it, Newcastle quickly became the North-East's centre of trade and commerce. In 1216, the town's rich merchants (or burgesses) were granted permission by King John to form merchant guilds and were allowed to appoint their own mayor and six aldermen. These guilds, of which there were initially twelve, were also known as 'mysteries', and were actually cartels formed within the different trades which restricted trade to guild members only.

An ever-expanding population now lived and worked in Newcastle and in the year 1400, in recognition of the town's growing importance, Henry IV made Newcastle a separate county within Northumberland. The Castle Keep and Castle Garth, however, remained crown property and part of Northumberland. As a result of this new arrangement, Newcastle's jurisdiction did not extend beyond the curtain wall and for a time, the Castle Garth became a sanctuary for the town's felons, an intolerable situation that was eventually resolved by legislation passed during the reign of Elizabeth I.

The main route to the north passed through Newcastle and twelve broad arches now carried an impressive stone bridge across the River Tyne, replete with a chapel, shops, houses and three defensive towers, one of which served as a gaol for petty criminals and vagabonds. To emphasise the town's growing sense of civic pride, two-thirds of the way across the bridge towards the Gateshead side, a large blue stone was set into the roadway. Marking the beginning of Newcastle's jurisdiction, the Blue Stone also determined the boundary with the Diocese of Durham and clearly defined the limits of its authority where the new county of Newcastle was concerned. The Blue Stone is housed in the Castle Keep today. To the east of the bridge, a broad stretch of the riverside had been reclaimed and the Quayside stretched from an open, triangular area known as Sandhill, on which the Close and the Side converged, to Sandgate, which marked the eastern boundary of the town walls.

By the end of the thirteenth century, Newcastle had become one of England's major ports. Ships and seamen from every port in Western Europe docked at the Quayside and the bustling waterfront had become a maze of tall, narrow warehouses, industrious workshops, over-populated dwellings and busy inns. Initially, the town's main exports were leather and wool, although the supply of raw materials could be seriously hindered by the intermittent turmoil that plagued the Anglo-Scottish border regions. There was also the nucleus of a shipbuilding industry on the riverside, as demonstrated in the late thirteenth century, when a substantial wooden galley was built in Newcastle for the fleet of Edward I.

By the fourteenth century, coal mined in the countryside around Newcastle was fast becoming the town's primary export and the main source of its wealth. The first recorded shipment appears to have taken place in 1305, and by 1378 some 15,000 tons of coal were being shipped out of Newcastle annually, destined for markets both at home and abroad. In return, an astonishing variety of merchandise from all over the world found its way into Newcastle, including weapons, armour, fine wine, silk, spices, furs, textiles and iron ore.

This hive of activity drew an ever-increasing number of townsfolk to the densely populated warren of timber-framed buildings that lined the sixteen narrow, congested alleys, or 'chares' as they were then known, that ran back from the riverside. The squalid and cramped conditions in which the majority of the populace existed were truly appalling. Due to the chronic lack of sanitation and close proximity of buildings, disease was rampant and fires were a constant hazard. In addition, two streams, the Lort Burn and Pandon Burn, which flowed down steep ravines through the town, were little more than open sewers choked with excrement, offal, decaying food and every other kind of refuse imaginable. High and low bridges crossed the Lort Burn, which flowed between Pilgrim Street and the Bigg Market and ran down present-day Dean Street to join the River Tyne at Sandhill. To the east, the Pandon Burn joined the river near Broad Chare, beside Sandgate.

Fifteenth-century progress

Many of the town's wealthier merchants conducted their businesses on the Quayside and in spite of the squalor, chose to live there, albeit in more salubrious and less claustrophobic circumstances. One of the town's most prominent merchants in the early part of the fifteenth century was Roger Thornton who resided in a substantial house on Broad Chare. Holding property in London and estates in Northumberland, Thornton was a model citizen and philanthropist who frequently served as mayor of Newcastle. He also built in 1412 the *Maison de Dieu* (commonly known as the Maison Dieu) or Hospital of St Catherine, on Sandhill, a charitable house for impoverished elderly or sick members of aldermen's families. The building was subsequently granted to the town by Thornton's son and from the sixteenth century onwards, the Newcastle Guild of Merchant Adventurers held their meetings in an upper room there, until a new guildhall was designed and built on this site by Robert Trollop in 1655. Roger Thornton is remembered, together with his wife Agnes and their fourteen children, in an exquisite brass plate that was commissioned on his death in 1429 and is now displayed in St Nicholas's Cathedral.

This brass plate depicting Roger and Agnes Thornton is displayed in St Nicholas's Cathedral. It was commissioned on his death in 1429. (Photo: Keith Durham.)

At some time during the fifteenth century, a group of seafarers formed a charitable guild for promotion of the interests of the growing maritime community and the relief of distressed seamen and their dependents. Originally named the Guild (or Brethren) of the Blessed Trinity, it formally came into being on 4 January 1505, securing some land on the Quayside for its base. A hall, chapel and lodging rooms were built on this site, which later expanded to include a schoolroom and almshouses for needy seafarers and widows. In 1536, Henry VIII gave this guild's work due recognition in the form of a royal charter, and at the same time the guild became an incorporated 'company' within the town of Newcastle-upon-Tyne. In 1753, Trinity House Nautical School was established which was staffed and run until 1870. Trinity House maintained lighthouses along the coast and in addition to all the Tyne ports, every harbour and landing stage from Whitby to Holy Island fell within its jurisdiction. It is still an active body, being one of the Guilds of Freemen of Newcastle-upon-Tyne.

Although the vast majority of Newcastle's domestic medieval buildings were destroyed in successive fires, or demolished in the nineteenth century, some examples from the period still survive. A few of the narrow chares still exist, in name at least, and on the Quayside at the bottom of the Long Stairs, is the striking medieval façade of the Cooperage. Parts of this building date from the fifteenth century and its tall, narrow aspect is a legacy of the cramped nature of the buildings that once lined the Close. The upper storeys were built with Dutch bricks, which had probably served as ship's ballast, and from the early eighteenth century, the premises were home to a cooper, who made wooden staved vessels. Opposite, on the riverfront, stands Number 35 The Close, one of the town's oldest timber-framed houses. Now housing The Quayside Pub, this building was once a prosperous, sixteenth-century merchant's premises complete with its own attached warehouse, and would have enjoyed direct access to the river.

Coal and wealth

In 1603, when James VI of Scotland came to the throne of England as James I, the constant threat of open warfare between the two countries eased considerably. Newcastle's role as a military base diminished even further, allowing commerce to become the driving force that established Tyneside as one of the most energetic and productive regions in the country.

By the mid-sixteenth century, Newcastle's coal trade had begun to expand rapidly and a group of powerful merchants had taken control of the mines and coal exports. Substantial shipments were sent on a regular basis to France and the Low Countries and London was burning all the coal Newcastle's ships could deliver. Over 30,000 tons of coal per year were being shipped out of Tyneside and by the end of Elizabeth I's reign in 1603, that figure had risen to over 160,000 tons. In the early part of the seventeenth century, Newcastle had a virtual monopoly on the export of coal with considerable control over rival ports like Sunderland. Its merchants were exporting almost 240,000 tons of coal per annum and by 1634, that figure had increased to 450,000 tons. Small wonder then that the well-known expression 'taking coals to Newcastle', meaning 'an utterly pointless exercise', was coined and first recorded in 1538!

Such was the town's importance at this time that it even began to rival London in its wealth. As Sir Timothy Eden quotes in his book *Durham*:

'the burgesses of Newcastle waxed fat and proud, believing themselves to be citizens not only of the richest town in the North but soon of the richest in England. They laughed and snapped their fingers at London herself: "Our staiths their mortgaged streets will soon divide!"'

The greatest part of coal was mined locally around Elswick, Benwell and Newburn, and on the south banks of the river were the thriving pits in Gateshead, Whickham and Winlaton. In order to avoid the time-consuming task of transporting such a bulky commodity across land, mining operations were kept as close to the River Tyne as possible. Wooden wagon-ways led to loading staithes on the riverbanks and droves of hardy miners toiled away in dangerous and ever-deepening shafts.

In the coal trade, nothing was wasted. Poorer quality coal that was mined locally could be used as fuel in the manufacture of glass and, at the beginning of the seventeenth century, a small glass-making industry emerged to the east of the town, on the Ouseburn. The venture flourished and, by the middle of the eighteenth century, Tyneside had become Britain's foremost supplier of window-glass. At North Shields, sub-standard coal was also used in the production of salt, which was created by heating and evaporating seawater in saltpans.

As already said, in those days the upper reaches of the Tyne could still be treacherous and masters of the large colliers that transported all this coal were unwilling to risk their ships by attempting to navigate too far upstream, preferring the safety of deeper anchorages at North and South Shields. As a result, coal had to be ferried downriver on keels. These were wooden, shallow-draught boats with pointed sterns, each capable of transporting around twenty-one tons of coal. The coal was loaded into the keel's hold from a 'spout' or riverside chute. The keel would then be taken downriver on the ebb-tide using oars, or sail if the wind was favourable. The keelmen who operated these keels were a proud breed and often competed for work by racing each other along the Tyne to the waiting ships. Their keels were taken alongside the waiting colliers where the crews would shovel the coal into the colliers, working long hours, even after darkness descended. This work was often very arduous, due to the difference in height between the keel's gunwale and the collier's deck.

The importance of their trade was acknowledged across Tyneside and in the early part of the sixteenth century they are mentioned in the town's Craft Guilds. In 1701, the Society of Keelmen was wealthy enough to erect an almshouse to accommodate members of its trade who were sick or had fallen on hard times.

Known as the Keelmen's Hospital, this fine, red-brick building, constructed in the Dutch style, still looks out over Sandgate, where many mariners, shipwrights and keelmen chose to live. In the mid-nineteenth century, however, when the river was dredged and deepened, colliers of all sizes were able to reach the staithes and the keelmen quickly became redundant. By 1872, the Society of Keelmen had ceased to exist, but to this day they are fondly remembered in the traditional Tyneside song, 'Weel may the Keel row'.

Every element of the coal trade was ruthlessly monopolised by Newcastle's wealthy merchants. They alone could trade and ship coal on the river and if it suited them, they would on occasion act as agents, or 'Hostmen', for outsiders wishing to buy or sell coal. These Hostmen, or 'Lords of Coal' as they were dubbed, were a powerful branch of Newcastle's Merchant Adventurers, who now held their courts in the new Guildhall, at Sandhill. This grand building, built on the old Maison Dieu site at Sandhill, was designed by Robert Trollop and opened in 1655.

Standing opposite the Guildhall, was a row of handsome, timber-framed merchants' houses. Two of these houses, Number 41 Sandhill (Surtees' House) and Number 44 Sandhill (Milbank House) were eventually united by John Clayton in the 1880s and became the building we know today as Bessie Surtees' House. Although parts of these buildings may date from the 1400s, the towering façade dates from the seventeenth century and is a fine and rare example of Jacobean domestic architecture. Each of the five storeys juts out slightly further than the one below, and along their full length are row upon row of small windows which must have given the merchant owners a fine prospect over the bustling Quayside. Much of the robust interior is oak-panelled and some of the rooms contain stuccoed ceilings and an abundance of elaborately carved decorations. Two of the finest buildings of their kind in Europe, Numbers 41 and 44 Sandhill are at present in the hands of English Heritage and well worth a visit.

The Surtees' house came to fame near the end of the eighteenth century after a scandal involving the wealthy owner's eldest daughter, a much-courted local beauty named Bessie Surtees. Not yet eighteen, Bessie fell in love with John Scott, a coal fitter who lived nearby. Their liaison was frowned upon and so, on a dark night in November 1772, the couple eloped, crossed the border to Blackshields in Scotland and were married under Scottish law. Shocking behaviour indeed, but as it turned out, the marriage was a happy one. John Scott went on to study law, became a barrister and in later life was created the first Lord Eldon, serving his country twice as Lord Chancellor of England. Newcastle's Eldon Square is named after him.

Plague and siege

By the seventeenth century, Newcastle was home to somewhere in the region of 12,500 people and was said to be *'the fairest and richest towne in England'*. But the town was destined to suffer some serious setbacks. In 1625, plague broke out in Newcastle and killed a great number of people. It struck again in the spring of 1636, brought in from Holland to North Shields and spreading from there to Newcastle, where over 7,000 people died in the most hideous way. The epidemic reached a peak in July 1636, beginning to wane towards autumn but leaving almost half the town's population dead.

Newcastle had barely recovered from that calamity when eight years later in February 1644, during the English Civil War, a Scottish army in alliance with the Parliamentarians laid siege to the town. A Royalist stronghold, Newcastle refused to surrender and Scottish gunners soon began pounding the town walls. Some of their artillery was sited across the River Tyne, on the banks of Windmill Hills at Gateshead, an elevation that gave the gunners an awesomely clear field of fire into the lower reaches of Newcastle and allowed them to cause great havoc and devastation in the town.

The siege dragged on for three months before the Scots launched a final assault on the beleaguered town. Eventually, in October 1644, they succeeded in breaching the walls and after much destruction and some hard dispute with the Royalists, took the town by storm. The Castle, however, had been re-fortified with bastions and artillery and the gaunt old Keep served as a final refuge for the town's mayor, Sir John Marley, and the remnants of his Royalist garrison. These defenders managed to hold the enemy at bay for a further two days before finally surrendering to the Scottish commander, the Earl of Leven.

The Scots were unwelcome visitors for the next three years and when they departed, the Parliamentarians began to govern the town. Because Royalist sympathisers owned many of Tyneside's mines and shipping, the trade in coal was severely restricted and almost ground to a halt. For a while the town's economy stagnated, but Newcastle's merchants, being canny and worldly-wise, played a waiting game and within fifteen years, Newcastle had regained much of its former panache. In 1660, Charles II was restored to the throne, the dour Parliamentarians were ousted from power and control of Newcastle's government was back in the hands of the Royalist merchants and Hostmen, amongst them Sir John Marley. The coal trade boomed once again and Tyneside's shipbuilding industry began to flourish.

Prosperity and improvements

At the end of the seventeenth century, Newcastle was once again a wealthy and important provincial centre and the town's recovered wealth and prosperity became increasingly reflected in its streets and architecture. In 1698, although the town's development was still restricted by its medieval walls, the traveller Celia Fiennes was moved to comment about Newcastle, that it: *'most resembles London of any place in England, its buildings lofty and large and of brick mostly and of stone, the streetes very broad and handsome'.*

One of these buildings must surely have been Alderman Fenwick's house, one the regions most elegant, seventeenth-century mercantile houses. Still standing today, it was one of a number of fine brick buildings that lined the lower part of Pilgrim Street, which was described by Celia Fiennes as *'the longest and fairest street in the town'.*

Not far from Fenwick's house, on present-day City Road, stands the Holy Jesus Hospital. Built by public subscription in 1681, this three-storey, brick building has Dutch gables, a large piazza and a decorative fountain. It was originally intended to support the less fortunate freemen of the town, their widows and any of their unmarried children. Strict rules governed the inmates of the hospital, including being locked in their rooms at 9 o'clock at night and having their doors unlocked again at 6 o'clock in the morning. No young children were allowed and the inmates had to attend church each week and take the sacrament. Each year they were given a free suit of clothing, a measure of coal and some pocket money if the charity allowed it.

Later on in Victorian times, the Hospital served as a soup kitchen but this was closed in 1891. In the 1960s, after standing empty for many decades, the Hospital was restored by the Museum Board as a museum to illustrate aspects of Newcastle's colourful history, with help from a generous bequest made by John George Joicey, a Gateshead businessman and owner of the mining company James Joicey & Co. Ltd, after whom the new museum was named. In 1993, the museum closed and all its interesting artefacts were taken to the newly-opened Discovery

Alderman Fenwick's house, later the Queen's Head Hotel and, more recently, the Newcastle Liberal Club. Purchased by Newcastle City Council in 1997, the building is now used as offices. (Photo: Graeme Peacock.)

Museum on Blandford Street. The Holy Jesus Hospital now houses the National Trust, which uses it as its base for the North-East Regional Office.

After Charles II died in 1685, his successor James II, in an attempt to promote Catholicism in the region, insisted that Newcastle's Corporation be elected solely from amongst the Catholic freemen. The townspeople vigorously rejected this imposition by electing a mayor of their own choosing and when James II fled in 1688, in the face of William of Orange's accession to the throne, the people of Tyneside greatly welcomed the news.

The Hanoverian dynasty, which began when George I came to the throne in 1714, was threatened the very next year when Jacobite sympathisers embarked on a rebellion to place James II's exiled son, James Francis Edward Stuart (frequently referred to as the 'Old Pretender') on the throne. Although many people in Northumberland flocked to the Jacobite banner, the town of Newcastle remained loyal to King George. The disorganised rebels were defeated by government troops at Preston. Thirty years later in 1746, when James Stuart's eldest son, Bonnie Prince Charlie, or 'the Young Pretender', retreated north to the defeat at Culloden, the town of Newcastle once again shrewdly stayed on the winning side and cheered on the Duke of Cumberland as he pursued the doomed Jacobite forces into Scotland.

Some believe this firm declaration of support for the Hanoverians is possibly where the nickname 'Geordie' originated but it has been pointed out that other townships, which also shunned the rebels, were not likewise named. As we shall see below, a more acceptable explanation will present itself in the mid-nineteenth century.

Although the lower reaches of the Lort Burn had been culverted in the last years of the seventeenth century, much of the area running down to Newcastle's

King Charles House, Shieldfield Green, Shieldfield, is the smaller house in the centre of the photograph where King Charles I was held prisoner at Newcastle by Parliamentarian forces. (© Newcastle Libraries.)

Sand Hill, 1836 by Thomas Allom.

Quayside still remained a grossly overpopulated ghetto of rickety, rat-infested tenements, lacking any sanitation whatsoever. By the eighteenth century, somewhere in the region of 28,000 people were living in Newcastle. Sandgate, in particular, teemed with the town's working classes and could barely contain its burgeoning population, a situation that was exacerbated by the continuous influx of outside labour. When the Methodist preacher John Wesley visited Newcastle in 1742, he was shocked to record that: *'so much drunkenness, cursing and swearing, even from mouths of little children, do I never remember to have seen and heard before'.*

The close proximity of such poverty, squalor and brutish behaviour led to the gradual withdrawal from the riverside of the town's wealthier residents, who chose increasingly to live in the upper reaches of the town, well above the Quayside. By the middle of the eighteenth century, the Age of Enlightenment had dawned in Newcastle, for them at least. Pleasant residential surroundings began to be constructed in the upper reaches of the town, such as Clavering Place and the elegant, Georgian-fronted dwellings at Hanover Square.

The eighteenth century also marked the beginning of the end for the town walls. In 1763, the first section to be demolished was that which ran along the Quayside and by 1812, little more remained of the medieval walls than can be seen today. Street lighting was introduced and oil lamps lit broad, new thoroughfares, such as Mosley Street, which linked Pilgrim Street to the vicinity of St Nicholas's Church and the Groat and Bigg Markets. Dean Street was created when additional stretches of the Lort Burn were filled in and this street ran down from Mosley Street to join the Side. Traffic and travellers crossing the medieval bridge, however, were still faced with a stiff climb in order to reach the upper parts of the town.

In 1771, such civic improvements were interrupted when, due to an abnormal amount of rainfall, the River Tyne rose nine feet above its usual level and completely flooded the Close, Sandhill and most of houses fronting the Quayside. It also swept away the central arches of the old medieval bridge, which by then had become a rather dilapidated structure and must have been something of an embarrassment to a town with such fine civic aspirations.

Within a year, a temporary wooden bridge had been constructed and in 1774 work was begun on a new stone bridge, which opened in 1781. This handsome structure was carried on broad stone piers, had nine wide arches and substantial abutments. Unfortunately, it also took up virtually a third of the waterway, and its arches were so low that only small boats could pass beneath it, a restriction that would eventually lead to it being removed to make way for the construction of the present Swing Bridge, less than a century later.

Two major churches were also built around this time. St Ann's was completed in 1768 on what is now City Road and was designed by William Newton, the man then generally regarded as Newcastle's first architect. Eighteen years later, the towering, elliptical All Saints' Church was erected on Lower Pilgrim Street, overlooking Dog Bank and Akenside Hill. Designed by the architect David Stephenson and completed in 1796, All Saints' Church replaced the medieval church of All Hallows and has become one of Newcastle's most striking landmarks and the third tallest religious building. Dominated by its elegantly-proportioned tower, the church is an exuberant expression of Classical architecture and one of very few oval-shaped churches in the country.

Social and cultural expansion

As the civic character of the town began to change, so too did the social and cultural aspirations of its residents. The *Newcastle Chronicle*, founded in 1764, was one of five newspapers that kept the population informed of both local and national events and a new Post Office made written communication somewhat more reliable. Banks were opened on Mosley Street and some buildings boasted fashionable shops on their ground floors with large windows displaying tempting merchandise imported from around the world.

For the upper echelons of society, there were concerts to applaud, elegant balls to attend and genteel house parties and soirées which proved very popular. William Newton was commissioned to design Charlotte Square and the town's Assembly Rooms, which stand nearby and were completed in 1776, while David Stephenson also designed the original Theatre Royal, which was built on Mosley Street and opened in 1788.

Those members of Newcastle's intelligentsia who took a keen interest in the arts, science and humanities established a Literary and Philosophical Society in 1793. It was founded as a 'conversation club' by the Reverend William Turner and others, more than fifty years before the London Library, with membership costing an annual subscription of one guinea. The club met in several Newcastle locations including the town's Assembly Rooms. The subjects of the conversations, and the books which supported them, were wide-ranging, but from the start such topics as religion and politics were prohibited. It was populated by the leading thinkers of the day who met to talk and exchange ideas.

The Society had an enterprising, liberal nature and the first women members had been admitted by 1804. Members were affluent enough to patronise a number of local craftsmen, among whom were the world-famous artist and wood engraver, Thomas Bewick, who had a studio near St Nicholas's Church, and the glass engraver, William Beilby, whose wonderful, enamelled-glass creations are still much sought after today. Speakers were often invited to give groundbreaking demonstrations of new technology, such as George Stephenson's miner's safety lamp in 1815. An important meeting took place under the Society's auspices in 1820 and established 'The Newcastle upon Tyne Society for the Gradual Abolition of Slavery in the British Dominions', and as we shall later see, the Society's lecture theatre was the first public room to be lit by electric light, during a lecture by Sir Joseph Swan on 20 October 1880. The Society thrived and in 1822 members decided to build themselves a permanent new home in the gardens of Bolbec Hall. The new building on Westgate Road was designed by John Green, and The Lit & Phil as we know it today was opened in 1825.

Meantime, Newcastle's government still remained in the hands of the powerful coal owners, merchants and shipping magnates who did much to further the town's progress, albeit in the process of making themselves wealthy. Among this select group of worthies were the Claytons, the Ridleys and the Blacketts, whose long-standing dynasties are celebrated in Newcastle's street names. To their credit, these more fortunate members of society also ensured that Newcastle's poorer citizens were not totally neglected and a number of charity schools were established in the town, together with an infirmary for the poor and a dispensary, where free medicines could be obtained.

Most of the groundwork was now in place for the next phase of expansion and at the beginning of the nineteenth century, Newcastle and Tyneside stood poised on the brink of an energetic era of invention, rapid industrial growth, civic improvement and social change that would transform the face of the region forever.

Grainger Town

In spite of the advances noted above, a somewhat archaic street pattern still existed within the very heart of Newcastle at the dawn of the nineteenth century. In particular, the layout between Newgate and Pilgrim Street remained essentially unchanged since medieval times and seriously hampered any further development. In the 1830s, however, three men, Richard Grainger, John Dobson and John Clayton, would between them fundamentally change the face of Newcastle forever.

Perhaps first and foremost of this shining triumvirate was Richard Grainger, for without his boldness, flair and vision, the town we admire today would simply not have existed. Born of humble parents in 1797, Grainger was a Tyneside builder and budding entrepreneur who quickly gained a reputation for work of quality. Shortly after completing a block of fine dwellings at Higham Place in 1820, Grainger married into a wealthy local family and, with his wife's financial backing, was able to fund an increasing number of successful building enterprises. These included a cluster of fashionable houses on Blackett Street and facing them, a three-sided development of imposing terraced houses named Eldon Square, which he completed in 1831. Grainger went on to build the Royal Arcade on Pilgrim Street in 1832 and followed up with a splendid, Regency style development at Leazes Terrace, designed by Thomas Oliver and completed in 1834.

On the Eldon Square project, Grainger had worked with an ambitious young architect named John Dobson, a former pupil of David Stephenson. In 1825, Dobson had submitted plans for a new town centre and although the town's corporation were already contemplating such a development, his efforts met with little enthusiasm. However, in 1834, the twelve-acre site between Pilgrim Street and Newgate, then known as Anderson Place, came up for purchase. Richard Grainger, realising the enormous potential of this prime location, grasped the opportunity and negotiated the purchase of the land and buildings, but he could not afford to develop the site himself.

Using a team of architects that included John and

John Dobson, 1787-1865.
(By kind permission of Linden Hall Hotel.)

Richard Grainger, 1797-1861.
(© Tyne & Wear Museums.)

Engraving of Grey Street from *Reid's Handbook To Newcastle Upon Tyne*, published in 1863.

Benjamin Green, George Walker, John Wardle, Thomas Oliver and John Dobson, Grainger submitted designs to the corporation for a new town centre to be built on the site, complete with broad streets, covered markets and a variety of shops and commercial buildings. Dobson had already submitted similar designs and been rejected, so Grainger realised that he needed someone with influence to encourage the corporation to accept the new designs. He was advised to move his legal account to the solicitor's firm run by John Clayton, the town clerk. Thus, Clayton became Grainger's advocate and legal adviser, and within two months the corporation had adopted his new plans and began to turn his dream into a reality.

The upper reaches of the Lort Burn were filled in and over this Upper Dean Street was built. The new street, running from Dean Street to Mosley Street and up to Blackett Street, effectively linked the Quayside to the town's centre. In 1836, this magnificent thoroughfare, which has been cited as the finest curved street in Europe, was re-named Grey Street in honour of Charles, Earl Grey, whose monument still dominates the centre of what afterwards became known as Grainger Town. Designed by local architects, John and Benjamin Green, Grey's statue crowns a 41-metre high Doric column erected in 1838 to commemorate the Great Reform Act of 1832, which was drafted during Earl Grey's term as Prime Minister.

Sweeping down from Grey's Monument in a broad elegant arc, Grey Street is a showcase of classical architecture and has along its length some of the finest buildings in Newcastle. Near the foot of the monument stands the triangular

Royal Arcade drawn by T. Allom and engraved by J. Sands in 1833. The Royal Arcade was designed by John Dobson for the developer Richard Grainger. A replica now replaces the original as the original building was taken down, to make way for Swan House Roundabout. Each stone was numbered with chalk and stored for rebuilding but alas the chalk washed off leaving a pile of unnumbered stones. (© Newcastle Libraries.)

block known as the Central Exchange, built by Richard Grainger in 1836-38, to the designs of John Wardle and George Walker. This triangular building was intended to be a corn exchange but instead became a subscription newsroom. The Central Exchange incorporates the glass-roofed Central Arcade, an Edwardian shopping arcade built in 1906, the interior of which features tasteful Burmantofts ceramic decorations. Opposite, on the corner of Hood Street, stands the Classical façade of what is now Lloyds Bank. At the time it was built, this structure was considered to be the epitome of a style that has become known as Tyneside Classical and is regarded by some as Grainger Town's finest building.

As Grey Street was developed, the old Theatre Royal on the corner of Mosley Street was demolished and in 1837, a new Theatre Royal was built on Grey Street. Designed by local architects John and Benjamin Green, this magnificent building, which features a towering Corinthian portico and an opulent auditorium, had its interior destroyed by a huge fire in 1899, but this was redesigned by Frank Matcham and the theatre re-opened on 31 December 1901. Externally, the building is exactly as it was when first built and nowadays, it regularly plays host to some of the finest performers and musicians in the world. While lower down, on the western side of Grey Street is the impressive façade of the building built by Richard Grainger in 1835 for the Bank of England. It is surely no accident of design that this magnificent building positively exudes formality and dignity.

Radiating westwards from the axis of Grey's Monument was Grainger Street, another broad thoroughfare, which ran to the Bigg Market and incorporated shop premises and a spacious, roofed meat market, designed by John Dobson. It was opened in 1835 and is known today as the Grainger Market. It was originally divided into two parts, the eastern section was a meat market, laid out in a series of aisles, and the western section, which was a vegetable market, constructed as a large open-plan hall. Leading off Blackett Street and running parallel with Grainger Street was Clayton Street, which crossed Newgate Street and linked up with Westgate Street (now Westgate Road). Lined with business premises, shops and dwelling houses, Clayton Street was also home to a new fruit and vegetable market, which faced the meat market on Grainger Street.

By 1840, Newcastle had one of the most elegant, accessible and sophisticated town centres in the land. Although the full extent of Grainger's vision was never quite fulfilled, in just a few short years he and his team of architects had transformed Newcastle's town centre beyond recognition and in the process, had achieved an aesthetic and commercial triumph.

The winds of change were also sweeping through other parts of Newcastle. Collingwood Street, which had been created in 1810, now linked Mosley Street

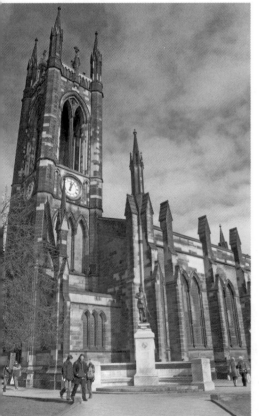

with Westgate Street and was lined with fine houses that incorporated shops on their ground floors. A network of sewers was constructed and toilets were installed in many of Newcastle's buildings. While in the Castle Garth an imposing Moot Hall, built in the Greek Doric style, now loomed above the houses and buildings on Sandhill. Down on the Quayside, Dobson added the now familiar collonaded fish market to the eastern corner of the Guildhall and in 1830, he went on to built St Thomas's Church in truly Gothic style at the Haymarket.

The Church of St Thomas the Martyr designed by John Dobson towers impressively above the Haymarket. The church was completed in 1830. Galleries were added in 1837, seating was replaced in 1881 and in 1972 the level of the high altar was lowered, the chancel screen removed, the chancel extended into the nave, with a nave altar. The church is a now a Grade II listed building. (Photo: Ian Scott.)

Tyneside's industrial age

In September 1825, the age of the railway dawned when George Stephenson, an engineer from Ovingham, in the Tyne Valley, built the first railway locomotive, which he called *Locomotion*, and, to great public acclaim, demonstrated it on a new railway line stretching from Stockton to Darlington. Stephenson had perfected his invention in the world's first purpose-built locomotive factory at 20 South Street in Newcastle, owned by a company set up by him and several others, and managed by his son Robert. Soon railway lines began to snake across the length and breadth of the country.

George Stephenson is one of the North-East's greatest sons and is honoured by a monument that can be found at the bottom of Westgate Road. Around the great man's feet are classical figures representing a navvy, a coal miner, a blacksmith and a locomotive engineer, each with an article pertaining to his trade. The monument, erected in 1862, was the work of John Lough, who was also responsible for the Collingwood Monument at Tynemouth. For Tyneside, the arrival of the locomotive would prove to be the catalyst that would transform the region into the industrial powerhouse of the North.

In 1844, George Hudson, the railway

Engraving of George Stephenson (1781-1848) from Smiles *Lives of the Engineers*. (© Newcastle Libraries.)

Locomotion, originally named *Active*, built in 1825 for the Stockton & Darlington Railway. (© Newcastle Libraries.)

financier who was dubbed 'The Railway King', brought his London line as far north as Gateshead and sought a site on which to build a railway station on the north side of the river. Eventually, land on Neville Street was chosen and in order to bring the railway directly into Newcastle's town centre, it was decided that a new bridge was required to cross the Tyne at a much higher level than the Georgian bridge. At that time, George Stephenson's son, Robert, was serving as a chief engineer in Hudson's empire and rather appropriately, it was he who designed the double-decker road and rail bridge that soared over 37 metres above the River Tyne, bypassing the Quayside and carrying the railway straight into the heart of Newcastle. For pedestrians and road traffic, the gruelling climb up from the Quayside was now a thing of the past.

Costing in the region of £500,000 to build, and paid for by various rail companies, the High Level Bridge was an engineering triumph of its time. Running from the foot of Wellington Street in Gateshead to the Castle Garth, and well over a quarter of a mile in length, the bridge was supported on towering stone piers and spanned by six cast-iron arches. The upper level of the bridge carried no less than three railway lines and from the lofty elevation of the lower level, pedestrians and equestrians were treated to hitherto unseen perspectives of Newcastle, Gateshead and the Quayside. Queen Victoria opened the bridge in September 1849 and returned in 1850 when the railway was officially welcomed into Newcastle with the grand opening of John Dobson's magnificent, neoclassical-style Central Station on Neville Street.

Road traffic and pedestrians began to travel across the High Level Bridge in ever-increasing numbers and St Nicholas Street was widened accordingly. Tyneside's booming industries needed extensive administrative support and

The Castle Keep, Old Tyne Bridge with High Level Bridge in the background. (© Newcastle Libraries.)

36

before long office blocks, such as those at St Nicholas Buildings, housed a growing number of shipping lines, legal establishments and insurance companies.

Sophisticated gas lamps now illuminated Newcastle's bustling streets, roads were macadamised and horse-drawn trams and carriages journeyed to and fro along the town's smart new thoroughfares. Newcastle was also fast becoming a major shopping centre. Crowds of fashionable customers strolled along rows of stylish new shops on Northumberland Street and in 1838, Emerson Bainbridge and his partner William Dunn opened a draper's and fashion shop in Market Street. In 1849, this housed twenty-three separate departments, making it what is believed to be the world's first general department store.

Meantime, the town of Newcastle continued to expand. In 1835, the outlying townships of Byker, Elswick, Jesmond, Heaton and Westgate had been formally incorporated into the town and, as Newcastle's population continued to increase, rows of substantial terraced houses began to appear on the quieter outskirts of the town. Properties in these leafy suburbs became much sought after by the city's middle and professional classes and areas such as Jesmond and Westgate Hill began to expand accordingly.

Unfortunately, the town's civic improvements did not extend to the Quayside. Since the building of the High Level Bridge in 1849, the area had become increasingly neglected and in the choked-up lanes and chronically overcrowded tenements, conditions were as squalid as ever. Houses were still devoid of sanitation or running water, and diseases such as smallpox, typhus and cholera regularly took their toll on the wretched inhabitants.

On 6 October 1854, fate took a hand when a fire on the Gateshead side of the river spread from a worsted factory to a warehouse containing nitrate sulphur and other combustible materials. The resulting explosions, which were heard as far away as Berwick, caused burning debris to rain down on Newcastle's Quayside, setting fire to ships,

Bainbridge dates back to 1838, and became the first department store in the world in 1849, after it began recording weekly turnover separately by department.
(© Newcastle Libraries.)

Great Fire of 6 October 1854, first published in *The Illustrated London News* of 14 October 1854. The sketch is from the High Level Bridge looking east towards the old Tyne Bridge, crowded with onlookers. Newcastle-upon-Tyne quayside (on the left) with the Gateshead quay warehouses engulfed by the inferno (on the right). (© Gateshead Libraries.)

warehouses and incinerating much of the medieval quarter. Both sides of the riverbank suffered extensive damage and most of the chares were completely burnt out. Over fifty people died, hundreds suffered horrendous injuries and many hundreds of families were left homeless. This area of Newcastle was later redeveloped, mostly for commercial use, and many of its people found new homes in the growing ranks of terraced houses overlooking the Tyne at Walker, Byker, Scotswood and Elswick.

More than ever before, the coal trade continued to be the driving force on Tyneside. Improved water-pumping techniques led to deeper, more productive mining operations and also allowed flooded pits that had been abandoned to be drained and re-opened. In 1815, George Stephenson had invented his safety lamp for miners and, although Sir Humphrey Davy's lamp was also available, Tyneside pitmen invariably opted for Stephenson's invention, thus earning themselves the enduring nickname 'Geordies'. Conditions underground, however, still remained perilous and the North-East's pits had more than their fair share of disasters.

Growth of shipbuilding

The advent of the railway now meant that vast quantities of coal could be transported rapidly overland to London, a development that inevitably signalled the demise of the tall-masted collier, which was still very much at the mercy of wind and weather. The question of coal transport to the London market now became a serious problem for the North country's colliery proprietors.

In order to compete with the railways, a coal merchant and entrepreneur named Charles Mark Palmer established a shipyard at Jarrow in 1851 and the following year, launched the *John Bowes*, a steam-powered, iron-built, screw-driven collier, which in a return trip of less than a week, was able to transport as much coal to London as a wind-propelled collier could manage in two months. Palmer's invention not only salvaged the transportation of coal by sea, but also proved to be the nucleus of a new shipbuilding industry on Tyneside. At the time of the Crimean War in 1854, Palmer's yard was producing rolled-armour plating for warships and had also secured a government contract to build the *Terror*, a 2,000-ton gunship.

Emerging Tyneside companies such as Clarke, Chapman & Company and Hawthorn Leslie & Company, which specialised in marine engineering, were essential to the shipbuilding industry, and in 1884, a talented engineer named Charles Algernon Parsons, who worked with Clarke, Chapman & Company at Gateshead, developed the steam-turbine engine. Parsons refined his invention and in 1889, went on to found his own company in Newcastle, C.A. Parsons & Company, which produced turbo-generators to his design. In June 1897, at Queen Victoria's Diamond Jubilee Fleet Review

John Bowes, the first steam collier launched from Palmers Yard, Jarrow 1852.
(© Ships' Collection: Newcastle Libraries.)

Sir Charles Parsons (1854-1931), inventor of the steam turbine. (© Newcastle Libraries.)

At the Spithead Review held off Portsmouth to commemorate Queen Victoria's Diamond Jubilee in June 1897, *Turbinia*, designed by Parsons and built in 1894 by Brown and Hood at Wallsend, attained the speed of 34 knots. (© Ships' Collection: Newcastle Libraries.)

at Spithead, off Portsmouth, his sleek vessel *Turbinia*, powered by his own turbine engine, amazed onlookers with a virtuoso performance at a speed of 34 knots, when the fastest Royal Navy ships using other technologies could only reach 27 knots. The *Turbinia* is now on display at Newcastle's Discovery Museum. By the turn of the century, Parsons' turbine engine would also prove vital in the newly-emerging electricity industry, when his invention allowed turbo-alternators to generate affordable electricity for millions of people across the world.

From 1895 onwards, Hawthorn Leslie & Company built a series of torpedo-boat destroyers at their Hebburn shipyard. In 1899, the company launched *Viper*, the world's first warship to be powered by the steam turbines developed by Parsons. This was the first turbine warship of any kind and achieved a remarkable 36 knots in sea trials. The company began to specialise in these small, fast warships and during the First World War, supplied twenty-eight of them to the Royal Navy.

Other yards, including Charles W. Mitchell's at Walker, were also building iron ships and in 1873, Mitchell had acquired a new yard at Wallsend, which was subsequently passed to his brother-in-law, Charles Swan. In 1880, after Swan's death, a Sunderland shipbuilder named George Burton Hunter formed a business partnership with his widow, and the world-famous shipbuilding firm of Swan & Hunter (later known as Swan Hunter) came into being. Under Hunter's dynamic leadership the firm of Swan Hunter began to expand and in 1897, acquired the Schlesinger David shipyard.

Initially, Swan Hunter confined itself to building colliers and barges, but in 1898, the company launched the first in a series of ocean-going passenger liners. In 1903, Swan Hunter amalgamated with Wigham Richardson's Neptune yard and three years later, the combined firm was able to build the prestigious transatlantic liner *Mauretania* which, at the time of her launch was the biggest ship ever built. For twenty years in succession, this luxurious passenger liner, which was powered by Parsons' steam turbines, held the Blue Riband award for the fastest Atlantic crossing and continued to ply the same route until 1934. The *Mauretania* was celebrated as a shining example of Tyneside craftsmanship and significantly reinforced the North-East's growing reputation as a world-famous centre of high-quality shipbuilding.

But without doubt, this monumental era of industrial expansion was dominated by one man, William George Armstrong (1810-1900), Tyneside's greatest engineer, inventor and entrepreneur. Armstrong was a qualified solicitor with a passion for engineering and in 1845, he became involved in a scheme to provide piped water from distant reservoirs to the households of Newcastle. He

QSPS *Mauretania* passing Low Lights, North Shields, at the mouth of the Tyne on her maiden voyage. (© Tyne & Wear Archives & Museums.)

Armstrong's Elswick Works, 1890s. (© courtesy BAE Systems.)

suggested to Newcastle Corporation that the excess water pressure in the lower part of the town could be used to power a hydraulic crane for the Quayside. He designed and built this and it proved so successful that Newcastle Corporation agreed to the installation of three more cranes on the Quayside. In 1847, Armstrong set up a business to manufacture cranes and other hydraulic equipment in a riverside factory at Elswick. Whilst continuing to produce cranes and other hydraulic equipment for docks and railways, the company expanded and soon branched out into bridge building, one of the first orders being for the Inverness Bridge, completed in 1855. By 1863, the number of men employed in his works had risen to 3,800.

Meanwhile, Armstrong had read about the difficulties the British Army had experienced in manoeuvring its heavy field guns during the Crimean War. He went on to invent a breech-loading field gun that was adopted by the armed forces. Rather than profit from his design, Armstrong surrendered the patent for the gun to the British government and was then employed as Engineer of Rifled Ordnance to the War Department. For his loyal services he was rewarded with a knighthood and in 1859 was presented to Queen Victoria.

Number 1 Gun, this five-pounder could be lifted out of its carriage by two or three men. (© courtesy BAE Systems.)

The Elswick factory continued to expand and became an important centre of armaments' manufacture. In 1867, Armstrong reached an agreement with Charles Mitchell, a shipbuilder in Low Walker, whereby Mitchell's shipyard would build the warships and Elswick would provide the guns. The first ship completed in 1868 was the gunship *Staunch*. Because it was impossible at that time for large ships to progress further upriver than Newcastle's low-slung, eighteenth-century, Georgian bridge, conditions were rather restricting for the Elswick works, which fitted the guns to ships built at Low Walker. Armstrong solved this problem by designing an innovative, hydraulic swing-bridge, which would replace the troublesome old Georgian structure. His own company built the wrought-iron superstructure and in July 1876, Tyneside witnessed the opening of the Tyne Swing Road-Bridge. Turning on a central pier through 180 degrees, the new bridge allowed sea-going vessels to navigate the eleven miles upstream to Armstrong's industrial complex at Elswick.

Armstrong now began to take an active interest in producing warships and in 1882, Armstrong's company joined forces with Mitchell's shipyard, to form Sir William Armstrong, Mitchell & Company Limited. In 1884, a shipyard opened at Elswick which would specialise in warship production. In 1885, Armstrong's Elswick Yard launched its first ship, *Panther*, a torpedo cruiser built for the Austro-Hungarian Empire. One year later, the Low Walker yard launched the *Glückauf*, which is generally regarded as the world's first successful oil tanker. The Low Walker yard also gained a reputation for building sturdy icebreakers, such as *Yermak* and *Baikal*, which were commissioned by the Russian government. The *Baikal* was destined for service as a train ferry on land-locked Lake Baikal in Siberia and as a consequence, the

Ice breaker *Baikal*, built on Tyneside, was dismantled, shipped to Lake Baikal in Siberia and re-assembled.
(© Newcastle Libraries.)

vessel had to be dismantled after completion on Tyneside and its component parts transported thousands of miles across Russia. It was then re-assembled on the shores of the lake under the supervision of men from the Low Walker shipyard.

By 1895, the Elswick Works was employing in excess of 13,000 men and in 1897, Armstrong merged with the firm of Sir Joseph Whitworth and the combined company became known as Armstrong Whitworth. The Imperial Japanese Navy became one of the Elswick shipyard's most important clients and at the Battle of Tsushima in 1905, warships and cruisers built at Elswick played a significant role in Japan's victory over the Russian fleet.

The firm spilled over into an adjoining factory at Scotswood, which specialised in the manufacture of munitions and by 1900, the company was employing 20,000 workers and occupied an extensive area along the banks of the Tyne. The rapid expansion of that area's population led to the replacement of the

The launch of HMS battleship *Invincible* at Elswick, 13th April 1907. (© Ships' Collection: Newcastle Libraries.)

bridge at Redheugh with a wider and more substantial structure in 1901. By 1914, one hundred and forty-one warships had left the Elswick yard, destined for navies across the world, fifty of them having been commissioned by the Royal Navy. At the Battle of the Falklands in 1914, one of these ships, HMS *Invincible*, was instrumental in sinking the German battle-cruisers, *Scharnhorst* and *Gneisenau*, before being sunk herself with great loss of life at the momentous Battle of Jutland in 1916.

The Armstrong-Whitworth FK.3 at their factory on Dukes Moor, Gosforth. (© courtesy BAE Systems.)

In 1913, Armstrong Whitworth began building military bi-planes in a factory near Gosforth and in 1917, had manufactured over one hundred Mark IV battle tanks, many of which saw action at the Battle of Cambrai. These tanks were the first in a long line of celebrated armoured fighting vehicles, including the battle tanks *Centurion* and *Challenger*, which were to see service all over the world. At the end of the First World War, the Armstrong Whitworth Company was employing a staggering 178,000 people.

Mark IV battle tank. (© courtesy BAE Systems.)

6
GATESHEAD'S EXPANSION

Gateshead, too, had its entrepreneurs and industrialists, albeit operating on a more modest scale. By the mid-1850s, small industries proliferated along the southern bank of the River Tyne and included paper mills, oil yards, rope manufacturers, glass companies, glue factories, clay-pipe makers, chemical factories and an alkali works, which at the time could boast the highest chimney in England. Tyneside was a major centre in the production of alkali, much of which was shipped to textile mills in the Midlands. At that time, this now virtually forgotten industry was of great importance on Tyneside and employed large numbers of people across the region.

A Gateshead industrialist of note was one George Hawks, who was the first mayor of Gateshead. At his works at Bottle Bank, he produced cannon balls, anchors, chains, picks, spades and tools. Hawks also owned the largest ironworks on Tyneside and from his foundry in Gateshead, supplied 5,000 tons of cast iron used in the construction of the High Level Bridge.

Throughout the nineteenth century, Gateshead was renowned for its exquisite Sowerby glassware, which was produced by Richard Sowerby and his son John at Sowerbys' Ellison Glass Works on East Street.

Gateshead also had its own funfair, known as 'the Hoppings', which was held on Windmill Hills, where a picturesque line of working windmills enhanced the fine prospect of Newcastle across the River Tyne. Over the years, some of the windmills gradually disappeared, but the unique panorama still remains.

Due to further dredging on the River Tyne, large colliers could now safely navigate as far west as Scotswood and in 1893, work commenced on the wooden staithes at Dunston, on the south bank of the Tyne at Gateshead. Over five hundred yards long and eventually completed in 1903, this massive timber structure was believed to be the largest of its kind in the world at that time. Along its length were a number of loading berths, each fitted with two spouts positioned

First mayor of Gateshead, George Hawks, (1801-63). (© Gateshead Libraries.)

Dunston Staithes opened in 1893 and continued to be used until the 1970s. It was restored for the 1990 Gateshead Garden Festival. (Photo: Keith Durham.)

at different levels. These spouts allowed coal to be loaded onto ships regardless of the tidal flow and, in its heyday, Dunston Staithes was handling well over 140,000 tons of coal a week.

During the nineteenth century, the thousands of men, women and boys employed in Tyneside's heavy industries worked long, gruelling hours, often in dangerous, polluted environments that simply would not be tolerated today. The majority of them lived in what became known as the 'Tyneside flats'. This type of dwelling first appeared in the 1860s and the Shipcote Estate in Gateshead, built by William Affleck in 1866, is thought to have been the first of these. They continued to be built in Tyneside from the 1870s until the outbreak of the First World War in 1914. These dwellings, with their paired front doors, were constructed in such a way that one family could live above another and yet, by a unique arrangement of internal and external stairs, both could enjoy the privacy of their own homes and backyards. Alongside a coalbunker, each backyard housed a toilet, commonly known as a 'netty'. The origin of the name is arguable, but most etymologists now agree that the origin of this word is in the English adjective 'needy', i.e. 'a place of necessity'.

'Tyneside flats', Hydepark Street, Gateshead. (Photo: Keith Durham.)

46

7
LIFE ON TYNESIDE

Because of their close proximity to one another, working folk on Tyneside developed a strong sense of community and these neighbourhoods became an integral part of the region's social fabric. By and large, wives stayed at home, bringing up families and performing minor financial miracles in order to keep hearth and home together. For those families without any means of transport, shopping for provisions on a regular basis in Newcastle's town centre was simply not practical. In time, a network of small corner shops spread across the suburbs, enabling thrifty housewives with limited budgets to make small, daily purchases of food and household necessities. If children were not at school, they played around the doors or roamed wherever they pleased, safe in a way that no longer seems possible in today's society.

Not surprisingly, recreation was as welcome then as it is now and within their social parameters, people enjoyed a variety of entertainment. Boat-racing on the Tyne attracted large crowds to the riverbank and world-champion oarsmen such as James Renforth (1842-71) and Harry Clasper (1812-70) were as feted in their time as footballers are today. Music halls became an increasingly popular diversion and in 1862, at Balmbra's Music Hall in the Cloth Market (now a popular pub with the same name), a composer and performer named Geordie Ridley belted out a song he had written called 'The Blaydon Races', which was destined to become Tyneside's favourite anthem.

Men enjoyed their beer, played quoits, cricket and billiards and gambled on bare-knuckle boxing contests, cock-fighting and other blood sports. Public executions had always been well-attended events and as late as 1829, hundreds of Tyneside families flocked to

The North of England Temperance Festival took place on the Town Moor and later became known as 'The Hoppings'.
(© Tyne & Wear Archives & Museums.)

the gallows on Newcastle's Town Moor to witness the hanging of Jane Jameson, (known locally as 'wor Jin'), a Sandgate woman convicted of her mother's murder and the first woman to be hanged in Newcastle for seventy-one years.

Horse-racing also drew large crowds from across the social spectrum, particularly the Northumberland Plate, an event first established in 1833, which was held on the Town Moor every June during Race Week. In 1882, the race was transferred to its present venue at Gosforth Park. The North of England Temperance Festival, initiated by the town fathers and held at the same time, took place on the Town Moor. The festival was a great success and attracted over 160,000 people, with sports, games, brass bands, military shows, football and cricket matches, in addition to a funfair. It was from this festival that Newcastle's annual funfair, known as 'the Hoppings' evolved, which remains a popular event to this day.

Local football matches were always well supported and in May 1892, teams from Newcastle's East End and Newcastle's West End football clubs merged to form Newcastle United, a phenomenon which was destined to draw the biggest crowds of all to its home ground at St James' Park. The club's distinctive black-and-white striped shirts were adopted in 1894 and the nickname 'the Magpies' soon followed. The origin of the name is disputed, but many fans attribute it to the black-and-white habit of a Dominican priest who was a regular supporter and became the club's unofficial mascot. The club went on to win its first FA Cup in 1910.

Photograph of the Newcastle v Sunderland derby match at St James' Park, Newcastle-upon-Tyne in 1904.
Lord Beresford, Admiral of the Channel Fleet, is about to kick off the match.
(© Amusements and Sports Collection: Newcastle Libraries.)

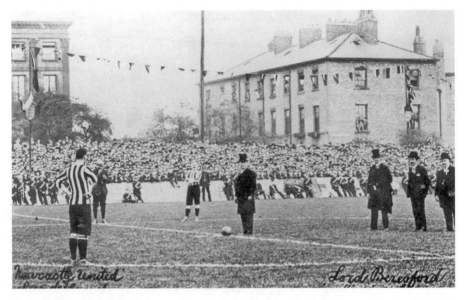

8
CITY OF
NEWCASTLE-UPON-TYNE

As the nineteenth century progressed, expansion continued apace in the town of Newcastle. In 1863, a Town Hall which incorporated the former Corn Exchange, designed by John Johnstone, was built on a triangular site at the foot of the Bigg Market. At the bottom of Westgate Road the ornate Union Club, now known as the Union Rooms, was completed in 1877. The economy continued to boom and an increasing number of older buildings were demolished to make way for banking premises and large Victorian office blocks, such as the Cathedral Buildings, which can be found in the vicinity of St Nicholas Street and Dean Street.

In 1867, Joseph Cowen, MP for Newcastle and proprietor of the *Newcastle Chronicle*, opened the Tyne Theatre and Opera House on Westgate Road, with an Italianate front and three tiers of balconies and boxes inside; this was to become a cinema in 1919, called the Stoll Picture House, before reverting to a theatre and opera house again. A General Post Office of truly classical style and proportions,

Below: The old Town Hall in the Bigg Market. (© Newcastle Libraries.)

Below: Tyne Theatre and Opera House on Westgate Road, still known by many as the Stoll Picture House. (Photo: Keith Durham.)

The General Post Office on St Nicholas Street which is now closed. (Photo: Ian Scott.)

boasting Roman Doric pillars below and Corinthian pillars above, was designed by James Williams and completed in 1874 on St Nicholas Street.

Nor were civic amenities neglected. In 1870, the Town Moor Improvement Act determined that two 35-acre sections of land would be developed for recreation, one to become Leazes Park and one at the Town Moor. Leazes Park is the city's oldest public park, lies to the west of the city centre next to the Royal Victoria Infirmary and opened its gates to the public in 1873. The central feature was the lake. Later, a bandstand and terrace were added and the whole park surrounded with metal railings, in the manner of other public parks at that time. The grand jubilee gates were added to commemorate the diamond jubilee of Queen Victoria and a palm house was also built there.

The park at Town Moor, called Exhibition Park, was the site for the Great Jubilee Exhibition of 1887, which was a huge success and attracted two million visitors. The only remaining item from the 1887 Exhibition now is the bandstand. The North-East Coast Exhibition was also held here from May to October 1929

Bandstand on the Town Moor recreation ground in 1870, now part of Exhibition Park. (© Newcastle Libraries.)

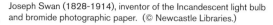
Joseph Swan (1828-1914), inventor of the Incandescent light bulb and bromide photographic paper. (© Newcastle Libraries.)

and was officially opened by the Prince of Wales on 14 May 1929. The exhibition was a symbol of the industrial success of the region and acted as an advertisement for local industry and commerce. During its twenty-four weeks of operation, a total of well over 4 million people attended. Remarkably, only seven criminal offences were recorded – six drunken offences and one for pick-pocketing! A massive fireworks display marked its closure on 26 October 1929. In the fullness of time, a boating lake, croquet lawns, tennis courts and other amenities were added to make this into a park to be enjoyed by Tynesiders of the early twentieth century.

May 1882 was an auspicious month, when the diocese of Newcastle was created from the northern portion of the diocese of Durham, the Church of St Nicholas finally became a Cathedral-church and the historic town of Newcastle-upon-Tyne was finally made a city. Around the same time, John James Fenwick, 'Mantle Maker and Furrier', opened his draper's shop at Number 5 Northumberland Street. A year later, the people of Tyneside acquired another delightful public park when Lord Armstrong gifted his estate at Jesmond Dene to the city. An iron, lattice-girdered bridge bearing his name still spans the Dene, and Armstrong Bridge is now the venue for occasional craft markets, weather permitting.

In 1884, the good people of Tyneside were able to marvel at a mind-boggling collection of exhibits from around the world when the Hancock Natural History Museum, named after the Victorian naturalist John Hancock, first opened its doors to the public. This museum opened on its current site when the collection of the Natural History Society outgrew its small museum on Westgate Road, and a major benefactor to the new museum was William Armstrong, who gave the then enormous sum of £11,500 towards its construction.

In addition to his other business interests, Armstrong had also become involved with an eminent physicist, chemist and fellow inventor named Joseph Swan. In 1860, Swan had developed a carbon-filament, incandescent lamp and in 1879, demonstrated an all-glass, hermetically-sealed light bulb, at Newcastle's Literary and Philosophical Club. This was the first practically usable, electric light bulb in the world. Swan's home in Gateshead was soon lit by electricity, as was Cragside, Armstrong's palatial dwelling at Rothbury. Together with Armstrong

Mosley Street became the first public street in Britain to be lit by Swan's electric lighting. (© Newcastle Libraries.)

and Charles Parsons, Swan established the Swan Electric Light Company at Benwell, the world's first electric light bulb factory, which in a merger in 1882, formed the Edison & Swan United Company, known as 'Ediswan'.

Swan went on to light up Mosley Street, which became the first public thoroughfare in Britain to acquire electric lighting. During this time, Swan also pioneered a dry photographic process that enabled permanent photographic prints to be made. This revolutionised the world of photography and became the basis of modern photographic film. Swan was honoured with a knighthood in 1904.

Lord Armstrong was one of Tyneside's most generous benefactors and in 1871, he was instrumental in founding the College of Physical Science, which offered instruction in mathematics, physics, chemistry and geology to meet the growing needs of the mining industry. This was subsequently renamed Armstrong College in 1904 and became the Newcastle Division of the University of Durham in 1908, thus forming the nucleus of the University of Newcastle-upon-Tyne, which was later created in 1963. Specialising in architecture, medicine, engineering and the Arts, the University has expanded over the years and built an enviable record of academic distinction. Lord Armstrong's last great project, begun in 1894, was the purchase and restoration of Bamburgh Castle on the Northumberland coast. He lived to see his vast, flourishing empire enter the twentieth century and died at Cragside in December 1900, at the venerable age of 90.

His generosity extended beyond his death and in 1901 his heir, William Watson-Armstrong, gave £100,000 for the building of the new Royal Victoria Infirmary in Newcastle. Originally founded as the Newcastle Infirmary in 1751, the RVI was opened on 11 July 1906 by Edward VII on ten acres of the Town Moor, a gift to the city by the corporation and freemen. This fully furnished and equipped hospital was ahead of its time, containing twenty wards, a nurses' home, chapel and five operating theatres, and guaranteed the welfare of Tynesiders into the future.

Tynemouth from the air. On the headland stands Tynemouth Castle, Priory and the Watch House. (Photo: © Graeme Peacock.)

North Shields Fish Quay and towering above, High Light. (Photo: © Graeme Peacock.)

Above: The Collingwood Memorial monument is situated so that it can be seen from the sea and the river. The four cannons on the walls flanking the steps came from his flagship *Royal Sovereign*, and were added to the monument in 1849, four years after its original completion. (Photo: © Graeme Peacock.)

On the south bank of the River Tyne in the historic Mill Dam area of South Shields stands the Customs House. (Photo: © Graeme Peacock.)

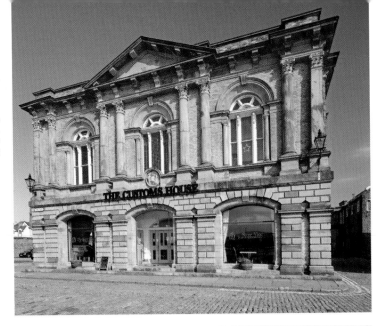

Wouldhave and Greathead Memorial, Ocean Road, South Shields. (Photo: © Keith Durham.)

Tyne, the second lifeboat to be built at South Shields. Launched in 1833 and serving for over 60 years, she saved over one thousand lives before being honourably retired in 1894. (Photo: © Graeme Peacock.)

St.Paul's Church, Jarrow has been a place of Christian prayer and worship for over 1300 years. The home of the Venerable Bede is now a centre of pilgrimage with international significance.
(Photo: © Graeme Peacock.)

Arbeia possibly means 'fort of the Arab troops'. The Roman fort at South Shields was first excavated in the 1870s. Pictured here is a reconstruction of the West Gate.
(Photo: © Keith Durham.)

Wallsend, looking west from the tower of the visitor centre over what was the Roman fort of Segedunum.
(Photo: © Graeme Peacock.)

Right: Newcastle's Castle Keep was built by Henry II between the years 1168 and 1178, within a site which also contains an early motte-and-bailey castle built by Robert Curthose, son of William the Conqueror; an Anglo-Saxon cemetery and the Roman Fort of Pons Aelius. One of the best examples of a Norman Keep in England, the Keep is a Grade I listed building. (Photo: © Graeme Peacock.)

Above: Castle Stairs which lead down to the river from the Castle Keep.
(Photo: © Keith Durham.)

Below: The Black Gate was added to the Castle between 1247 and 1250, forming an additional barbican in front of the earlier north gate of the castle.
(Photo: © Graeme Peacock.)

The Cloisters, Blackfriars Friary. Much of the Dominican monastery has now been demolished.
(Photo: © Graeme Peacock.)

The site of the Holy Jesus Hospital has been in use for 700 years helping the people of Newcastle. On the site stood an Augustinian friary dating to the thirteenth century, then an almshouse for retired freemen. A soup kitchen was built next to almshouse in the nineteenth century, before the site was acquired as a working office.
The building is used now as the base for the National Trust's North-East Regional Office.
(Photo: © Graeme Peacock.)

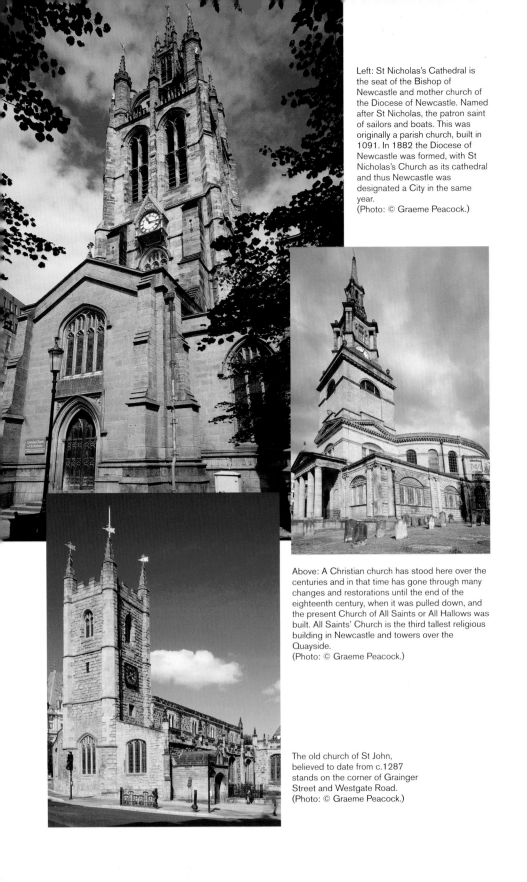

Left: St Nicholas's Cathedral is the seat of the Bishop of Newcastle and mother church of the Diocese of Newcastle. Named after St Nicholas, the patron saint of sailors and boats. This was originally a parish church, built in 1091. In 1882 the Diocese of Newcastle was formed, with St Nicholas's Church as its cathedral and thus Newcastle was designated a City in the same year.
(Photo: © Graeme Peacock.)

Above: A Christian church has stood here over the centuries and in that time has gone through many changes and restorations until the end of the eighteenth century, when it was pulled down, and the present Church of All Saints or All Hallows was built. All Saints' Church is the third tallest religious building in Newcastle and towers over the Quayside.
(Photo: © Graeme Peacock.)

The old church of St John, believed to date from c.1287 stands on the corner of Grainger Street and Westgate Road.
(Photo: © Graeme Peacock.)

Left: Completed in 1701, The Keelman's Hospital was for sick and aged keelmen and their families. The keelmen agreed to contribute one penny a tide from the wages of each keel's crew and Newcastle Corporation made land available in Sandgate. (Photo: © Graeme Peacock.)

Below: Hidden away off Broad Chare on the Newcastle Quayside is Trinity House. Its buildings date back to 1505 when a hall, chapel and lodging rooms were built and later expanded. Trinity House is a working maritime organisation, incorporated by Royal Charter since 1536. (Photo: © Keith Durham.)

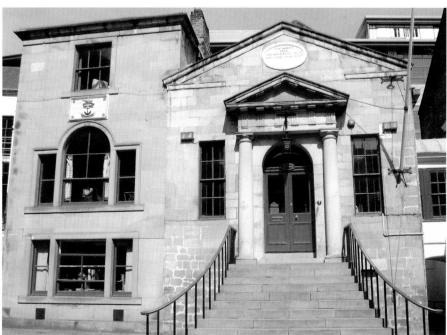

Sandhill, Newcastle Quayside, from the Tyne Bridge depicting Bessie Surtees House, centre. A fine example of Jacobean domestic architecture, this merchant's house is best known as the scene of the elopement of Bessie with John Scott, later to become the first Lord Eldon, Lord Chancellor of England. (Photo: © Graeme Peacock.)

To the Right Worshipful John Erasmus Blackett Esq.r Mayor of Newcastle upon Tyne, This VIEW of the RUINS of the BRIDGE of that TOWN, as they appeared after the fall thereof in November 1771. Is most respectfully Inscribed by his very obliged and most devoted faithful humble Servant John Brand. October 5.th 1771

A copy of an etching of the Tyne Bridge in 1771. It shows the Bridge after the floods of 1771. The fifth, seventh, eighth and ninth arches have collapsed, taking shops and houses with them. This Bridge was possibly built in the late twelfth century, rebuilt after the fire of 1248 and repaired several times before suffering this flood damage in 1771. (© Bridges Collection: Newcastle Libraries.)

'Keelmen heaving in coals by moonlight' 1835. Oil on canvas, 92.4 x 122.9 cm (36 3/8 x 48 3/8 inches), by Joseph Mallord William Turner (1775-1851). This painting is displayed in the National Gallery of Art, Washington, DC.

The Guildhall on the Sandhill was the ancient centre of municipal government of Newcastle. There is evidence of the existence of a guildhall as early as the 13th century. Robert Trollop designed and built a new Guildhall in 1655 and much of his work survives inside the building. In 1823 John Dobson added the colonnaded rounded east end to the building. (Photo: © Graeme Peacock.)

The Assembly Rooms were built by subscription, begun on 19 August 1773 and opened in race-week, June 1776. (Photo: © Graeme Peacock.)

The Moot Hall was built in a Greek Doric style with columned portico to the front, the rear is based on the Parthenon in Athens. It was the first court in the country to be licensed to hold civil weddings and other ceremonies, and is also used for school and university Mock Trial Competitions. (Photo: © Graeme Peacock.)

Designed by John Dobson, Grainger Market opened in 1835 and was once the largest covered market in the country. It was part of the 19th century redevelopment of the city to replace markets on the site of Grey Street. Grainger Market is a Grade I listed building. (Photo: © Graeme Peacock.)

Designed by architect Thomas Oliver, and built in 1830 by Richard Grainger, Leazes Terrace is one of the best examples of terraced residences in the country. The University of Newcastle-upon-Tyne uses a large part of the terrace as Halls of Residence. Leazes Terrace is now a Grade I listed building. (Photo: © Graeme Peacock.)

The Central Arcade was originally used as a commercial exchange and newsroom, and later as an art gallery. Built by Richard Grainger in 1836-38 to the designs of John Wardle and George Walker, it was rebuilt in 1906 after a fire, at which time the present Central Arcade was formed to cut through from Grey St to Market St, with a link to Grainger St. Today the Arcade houses a number of interesting retail outlets..
(Photo: © Graeme Peacock.)

In 1879 Joseph Swan demonstrated his electric light bulbs at the Lit and Phil which became the first public building to be illuminated. by electric light.
(Photo: © Science Museum).

Left: The Literary and Philosophical Society of Newcastle-upon-Tyne (Lit & Phil) is the largest independent library outside London. Founded in 1793 as a 'conversation club' by the Reverend William Turner and others with an annual subscription of one guinea. Members debated a wide range of issues, but religion and politics were prohibited. This building was designed by John Green and built between 1822 and 1825 on Westgate Road. The building is still in use today, with many original features including iron-work second-floor galleries. Alexander Armstrong, actor, comedian and host of BBC's quiz show *Pointless*, strongly supports the Lit & Phil and became its president in February 2011.
(Photo: © Graeme Peacock.)

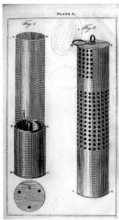

Safety lamp invented by George Stephenson in 1815 for use in mines.
Taken from 'Report Upon the Claims of Mr. George Stephenson, Relative to the Invention of His Safety Lamp, by the Committee Appointed at a Meeting Holden in Newcastle November 1st 1817', an original tract held in the North of England Institute of Mining and Mechanical Engineers.

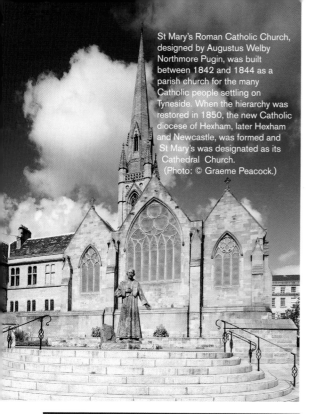

St Mary's Roman Catholic Church, designed by Augustus Welby Northmore Pugin, was built between 1842 and 1844 as a parish church for the many Catholic people settling on Tyneside. When the hierarchy was restored in 1850, the new Catholic diocese of Hexham, later Hexham and Newcastle, was formed and St Mary's was designated as its Cathedral Church.
(Photo: © Graeme Peacock.)

The statue of Cardinal Basil Hume (above) is situated in front of the Cathedral and was unveiled by Queen Elizabeth II on 7 May 2002. It shows Cardinal Hume in his Benedictine monk's habit, wearing a cardinal's skull cap and the cross of St Cuthbert. (Photo: © Ian Scott.)

Left: The magnificent Cathedral Buildings on Dean Street, leading down from Grey Street to the Quayside. These were built circa 1900. (Photo: © Graeme Peacock.)

Above: The workshops of artist, wood engraver and and naturalist Thomas Bewick (1753-1828), is marked by this bust of Bewick on the side of Milburn Buildings in the churchyard of St Nicholas's Cathedral. (Photo: © Keith Durham.)

Above: The Theatre Royal is a Grade I listed building situated at the top of Grey Street. Designed by local architects John and Benjamin Green as part of Richard Grainger's grand design for the centre of Newcastle, it was opened in February 1837 with a performance of *The Merchant of Venice*.
(Photo: © Graeme Peacock.)

Left: Lloyd's Bank Building. Lloyd's Bank has resided in this Grade II listed building since 1908. It is regarded by some as Grainger Town's finest building.
(Photo: © Keith Durham.)

Left: Grey Street was built by John Dobson and Richard Grainger in the 1830s. The street runs south from Grey's Monument to the junction with Mosley Street, then continues as Dean Street following the route of the Lort Burn which runs underneath Grey Street and Dean Street. Grey Street was voted 'Best street in the UK' by BBC Radio 4 listeners in 2002.
(Photo: © Graeme Peacock.)

Grey's Monument stands at the head of Grey Street. Erected to Charles Grey, 2nd Earl Grey in 1838 for the passing of the Great Reform Act of 1832. It consists of a statue of Lord Grey standing atop a 40m high column. The column was designed by local architects John and Benjamin Green.
The statue of Earl Grey was created by the sculptor Edward Hodges Baily and lost its head when it was struck by lightning. In 1941 a new head was sculpted by Roger Hedley (son of artist Ralph Hedley). Grey's Monument is a Grade I listed monument.
(Photo: © Graeme Peacock.)

Above: Emerson Chambers, a Grade II listed building standing on Blackett Street, is an example of Art Nouveau architecture. Designed by Benjamin Simpson in 1903, it boasts views of Grey's Monument and Grey Street.
(Photo: © Graeme Peacock.)

Newcastle Central Station was designed by John Dobson and constructed in collaboration with Robert Stephenson (also responsible for the High Level Bridge) between 1845 and 1850. The opening ceremony, attended by Queen Victoria, took place on 29 August 1850. The railway station is connected to the Tyne & Wear Metro underground which runs underneath the station. It is a Grade I listed building. An ambitious major redevelopment of the portico was completed in April 2014, which provided glazed arches for weather protection outside the station and doubled the size of the retail areas inside. (Photo: © Graeme Peacock.)

Founded in 1751 as the Newcastle Infirmary, the Royal Victoria Infirmary (RVI) was opened on 11 July 1906 by Edward VII. Queen Victoria's statue was the gift of Sir Riley Lord, who was knighted for his efforts in getting the Infirmary built. The new Victoria Wing, opened in 2010, houses a state-of-the-art Accident and Emergency Department and a Children's hospital. The RVI is a major teaching hospital, closely linked with the Faculty of Medical Sciences at Newcastle University. (Photo: © Graeme Peacock.)

The Armstrong Building is on the site of the original Armstrong College of Physical Science founded in 1871, renamed Armstrong College in 1904 and became the Newcastle Division of the University of Durham in 1908. In August 1963 by an Act of Parliament, the University of Newcastle-upon-Tyne was born. (Photo: © Graeme Peacock.)

The Hancock Natural History Museum, named after the Victorian naturalist John Hancock opened in 1884. The collections are owned by the Natural History Society of Northumbria, but it is managed by Tyne & Wear Archives & Museums on behalf of Newcastle University. In 2006 it merged with Newcastle University's Hatton Gallery to form the Great North Museum and after a major extension and refurbishment of the original Victorian building, the museum reopened in 2009 as the Great North Museum: Hancock. (Photo: © Ian Scott.)

After a petition by 3,000 working men of the city for 'ready access to some open ground for the purpose of health and recreation', Leazes Park was established in 1873. (Photo: © Ian Scott.)

Another green space in Newcastle is the Town Moor, lying immediately north of the city centre. The freemen of the city have the right to graze cattle on it. The Exhibition Park is located on the south-eastern corner where the pavilion built for the North-East Coast Exhibition of 1929 stands. The building, originally a temporary structure, housed the Newcastle Military Vehicle Museum from 1983-2006, but had to be closed because of structural problems. (Photo: © Ian Scott.)

Jesmond Dene is a public park that follows the river Ouseburn between South Gosforth and Jesmond Vale. Laid out during the 1860s by Lord Armstrong and his wife of Jesmond Dene House, the design is intended to reflect a rural setting and is home to exotic trees, wildlife and many woodland birds, notably the kingfisher. (Photo: © Keith Durham.)

Opened in 1878, and donated to the people by Lord Armstrong, Armstrong Bridge spans the ravine of the Ouseburn. It is said that Lord Armstrong had the bridge built because his wife Margaret was unhappy to see horses struggle to pull the carts and carriages from East Jesmond into Jesmond and Newcastle. The bridge is closed to traffic today and is now a venue for occasional craft markets. (Photo: © Keith Durham.)

The Bee Hive Hotel, one of the many public houses to be found in the Bigg Market which has become well known for party revellers. The term 'bigg' refers to a type of coarse barley that used to be sold in this market.
(Photo: © Graeme Peacock.)

Above: Originally sited in St Nicholas's Square but moved to the Bigg Market to make way for a grand statue of Queen Victoria in 1903, this drinking fountain dated 1894, is dedicated to Dr J H Rutherford, a preacher, doctor, educationalist and a friend to the poor.
Ironic that a inscription on one of the panels has the legend 'Water Is Best' as it is sited in the area that is world famous, or infamous, for its bars and fun-pubs.
(Photo: © Keith Durham.)

Below: Balmbras Music Hall, Cloth Market, now a Grade II listed building, is where the song 'The Blaydon Races' was first performed by George 'Geordie' Ridley in 1862. The song actually refers to this music hall as the starting point for the trip to the races. (Photo: © Ian Scott.)

Newcastle's major shopping street, Northumberland Street, now pedestrianised, is the most expensive place per square metre to own a shop outside London. The most famous shop on the street is Fenwick Department Store, renowned locally for its annual Christmas window display. (Photo: © Ian Scott.)

Designed by John Dobson, Eldon Square is a public square built on three sides and open on the south side to Blackett Street. It was part of the 1825–40 reconstruction of Newcastle city centre. In the 1960s the west and north terraces around the square were demolished to be replaced by part of Eldon Square Shopping Centre which now dominates what now is called Old Eldon Square. In the centre of the grass space is the site of the war memorial and the location for the city's Remembrance Day commemorations. (Photo: © Graeme Peacock.)

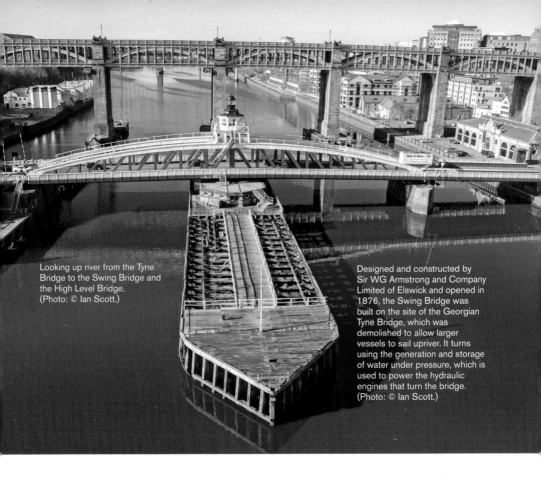

Looking up river from the Tyne Bridge to the Swing Bridge and the High Level Bridge. (Photo: © Ian Scott.)

Designed and constructed by Sir WG Armstrong and Company Limited of Elswick and opened in 1876, the Swing Bridge was built on the site of the Georgian Tyne Bridge, which was demolished to allow larger vessels to sail upriver. It turns using the generation and storage of water under pressure, which is used to power the hydraulic engines that turn the bridge. (Photo: © Ian Scott.)

Below: Opened in 1849, the High Level Bridge is the oldest of the existing bridges that cross the Tyne Gorge. The need arose for a railway bridge to link the south of England with Newcastle and Edinburgh. The dual road (lower deck) and rail bridge (upper deck) was designed by Robert Stephenson. This image shows the elegant curve of the bridge and the height it towers above the Quayside. (Photo: © Ian Scott.)

The walkway and the wrought-iron work of the Bridge's lower deck. (Photo: © Ian Scott.)

Known the world over, the iconic Tyne Bridge connects Pilgrim Street in Newcastle with the High Street in Gateshead. The bridge was designed by the engineering firm Mott, Hay and Anderson, and built by Dorman Long and Co. of Middlesbrough. The bridge was opened by HM King George V in 1928. (Photo: © Graeme Peacock.)

Above: Tyne Bridge, framing Sage Gateshead, Baltic Centre for Contemporary Art and Gateshead Millennium Bridge. (Photo: © Graeme Peacock.)

Opened in 1870 at the bottom of West Street stands Gateshead's third Town Hall after the previous building on Wellington Street was demolished to make way for the new railway line to the High Level Bridge. As well as council offices, the old Town Hall housed a police station, magistrate and county courts and police cells, which can still be seen today. (Photo: © Graeme Peacock.)

Below: Within Saltwell Park sits the Gothic-style mansion Saltwell Towers, a Grade II listed building, designed and built for his family by leading stained-glass master craftsman and manufacturer, William Wailes. The estate was left to Gateshead corporation in 1878, but William Wailes continued to live there until his death in 1881.

Saltwell Park is also known as 'The People's Park', a name that is still used by locals. Designed by Edward Kemp, it was opened to the public in 1876. Since its restoration between 1999 and 2005, it has won a host of awards, including 'Britain's Best Park' in 2005. In 2013 it was relisted as one of fifty-five Green Heritage sites in the UK. (Photo: © Graeme Peacock.)

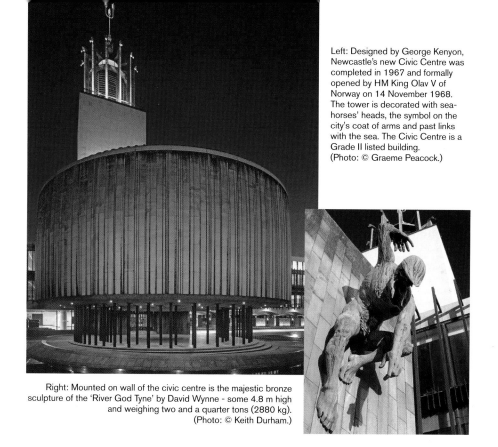

Left: Designed by George Kenyon, Newcastle's new Civic Centre was completed in 1967 and formally opened by HM King Olav V of Norway on 14 November 1968. The tower is decorated with sea-horses' heads, the symbol on the city's coat of arms and past links with the sea. The Civic Centre is a Grade II listed building.
(Photo: © Graeme Peacock.)

Right: Mounted on wall of the civic centre is the majestic bronze sculpture of the 'River God Tyne' by David Wynne - some 4.8 m high and weighing two and a quarter tons (2880 kg).
(Photo: © Keith Durham.)

Tom Collins House, Byker Wall Estate, The Byker Wall was designed by architect Ralph Erskine, assisted by executive architect Vernon Gracie and completed in 1981. The Wall has been cited as an example of enlightened town planning and is on UNESCO's list of outstanding twentieth-century buildings. In January 2007, the Byker Estate of which the Wall forms a part, was given Grade II listed building status. (Photo: © Keith Durham.)

Opened on 11th November 1982 to a design by Ove Arup and Partners, the S-shaped Byker Metro Bridge carries the Metro Rapid Transit System over the Ouseburn between Manors and Byker stations. It has a total length of 815m and width of 8.2m., carrying standard gauge double tracks up to 30m above the ground. It is one of three viaducts that cross the Ouseburn linking Byker with Newcastle city centre.
(Photo: © Graeme Peacock.)

Opened on 6 November 1981 by the Queen, the Queen Elizabeth II Metro Bridge carries the Tyne and Wear Rapid Transit Metro trains across the river Tyne. In 2006 Nexus, who operate the system, commissioned artist Nayan Kulkarni to install a huge artwork using the bridge as his canvas.
The artwork, *Nocturne* using LED lighting, is Britain's biggest illuminated artwork.
(Photo: © Ian Scott.)

St James' Park is the home of Newcastle United F. C. since 1892. It has changed beyond recognition since the early 1990s when local businessman Sir John Hall took over the club and developed the ground into a 52,405 all-seater stadium. (Photo: © Graeme Peacock.)

The Chinese Arch on St Andrew's Street welcomes you to Chinatown. Built in 2004 by Shanghai craftsmen, the Arch stands 11 metres tall and is flanked by two Chinese guardian lions facing St James' Park football ground. Chinatown lies within the historic Grainger Town, mainly on Stowell Street. Behind the buildings on the north side of Stowell Street marking the northeast boundary of the district, runs one of the best parts of the original Town Walls. (Photo: © NewcastleGateshead Initiative.)

Newcastle's Quayside has had a spectacular transformation since the sixties and seventies. The Newcastle Law Courts, restaurants, bars, night clubs, hotels and expensive apartment blocks now replace the steel sheds and bonded warehouses which once occupied the Quayside and the adjoining streets.

Above: The Law Courts were designed by local architects Napper Collerton. Built of red sandstone from Dumfriesshire, these buildings provide ten crown courts and three county courts. (Photo: © Graeme Peacock.)

Left: 'The Swirl Pavilion' by Raf Fulcher 1998, is named after a hidden stream that runs into the Tyne at this point. The towns carved around the inner rim are the destinations found on the sign of a local shipping company. (Photo: © Graeme Peacock.)

Below: 'The Blacksmith's Needle', designed by Alan Dawson, was made from forged steel by members of the British Association of Blacksmith Artists (BABA) at a series of forging sessions around the country. Conical in form, with six sections each containing objects with a maritime theme relating to one of the senses, it was inaugurated in May 1997 by Evelyn Glennie, the percussionist, who rang the bell hanging inside the Needle. (Photo: © Graeme Peacock.)

Gateshead Millennium Bridge for pedestrians and cyclists. Designed by architects Wilkinson Eyre and structural engineers Gifford & Partners, it was opened to the public on 17 September 2001, and dedicated by Queen Elizabeth II on 7 May 2002. The bridge is also known as the 'Blinking' or 'Winking Eye' Bridge because of its shape and tilting mechanism.
(Photo: © Graeme Peacock.)

Above: Dutch floating crane, *Asian Hercules II,* positioning the Gateshead Millennium Bridge in its resting place between the Gateshead and Newcastle quaysides on 20 November 2000. (Photo: © Graeme Peacock.)

Right: The Baltic Flour Mills was built for Joseph Rank Limited in 1950 as a dual purpose factory producing flour and animal feed. The factory has now been turned into Baltic Centre for Contemporary Art, which opened its doors in 2002. It hosts a frequently changing programme of exhibitions and events, and in 2011 was the venue for the Turner Prize exhibition, attracting nearly 150,000 visitors.
(Photo: © Graeme Peacock.)

The panoramic hilltop of a reclaimed former colliery pithead baths near the A1 was chosen as the location of the 'Angel of the North', so that it could be seen from a distance. The 'Angel' was designed by sculptor Sir Antony Gormley and rises 20 metres (66 ft) from the ground, dwarfing all who come to see it. Completed in February 1998, the 'Angel' is made from 200 tonnes of steel, with a wingspan of 54 metres (177 ft). It's seen by one person every second – that's 90,000 every day or 33 million every year! (Photo: © Graeme Peacock.)

'Designed by Foster and Partners, Sage Gateshead is a radical design based on the curve of the Tyne Bridge. Opened to the public on 17 December 2004, beneath its stainless steel roof are three separate performance spaces, five bars, a brasserie, the 'Sir Michael Straker Café' and a multi-purpose function room. It hosts concerts from internationally famous artists and orchestras and is also home to the renowned Royal Northern Sinfonia. (Photo: © NewcastleGateshead Initiative.)

Viewed from the Newcastle quayside, Sage Gateshead towers above the Gateshead quayside like a giant armadillo. (Photo: © Keith Durham.)

Eldon Square, the War Memorial and the new 'intu Eldon Square' shopping complex. The entrance leads through to shops and the indoor Eldon Square bus station which was opened in 2007. (Photo: © Ian Scott.)

Designed by John Dobson circa 1841, the former Market Keeper's Office and Toll House, complete with clock tower, stands in the centre of Times Square. The Square was originally the site of the old livestock market which traded around 10,000 animals each week. The offices of toll collector and market keeper were located on the ground floor of the building, while the upstairs held accommodation for both of their families. (Photo: © Ian Scott.)

Below: Times Square, the first new public square in Newcastle for over a century, houses the International Centre for Life, which combines Newcastle University's Genetics department, a Bioscience Centre, and the Life Science Centre visitor attraction, featuring science workshops and a varied programme of events for young and old all year around. The DNA helix created by Charles Jencks was commissioned by the International Centre for Life in 2000. It stands next to the Market Keeper's House in Times Square.
(Photo: © Graeme Peacock.)

Northumbria University City Campus East, home to the School of Design, School of Law and the Newcastle Business School (NBS). NBS and Law are housed in one building, and the School of Design is across a courtyard. The buildings have won design awards since opening in September 2007 and are now a Newcastle landmark. (Photo: © Graeme Peacock.)

Left: On St James's Boulevard stands Citygate Campus, part of the Newcastle University Business School. (Photo: © Graeme Peacock.)

Below: St James's Boulevard links central Newcastle to Gateshead via the Redheugh Bridge and the Gateshead Western Bypass. (Photo: © Ian Scott.)

9

TWENTIETH-CENTURY GATESHEAD

Across the river, Gateshead continued to thrive and in 1889, became a county borough. The bustling town centre could boast some fine civic buildings including a handsome town hall, designed by John Johnstone, built on West Street and opened in 1870. Gateshead was also home to William Wailes, an artist and entrepreneur specialising in stained-glass design, who bought the Saltwell Estate in Low Fell in 1860. He landscaped the grounds and built the neo-Gothic extravaganza known as Saltwell Towers as his home. However, Wailes experienced financial difficulties and in 1876, Gateshead Corporation purchased the parkland and transformed it into one of the finest public parks in the North-East. But one of Wailes's conditions was that he retained the right to live in Saltwell Towers until his death in 1881.

In 1884, 'The Towers' as it was known was leased to Joseph Shipley, a solicitor and avid art collector who lived there until his death in 1909. Shipley bequeathed his vast collection of paintings and sufficient money to build an art gallery to the City of Newcastle. However, a difficult clause in his will eventually led to Newcastle's rejection of the bequest and it was then offered to Gateshead Municipal Council, together with the money to build the art gallery. A selection of paintings from Shipley's collection is now displayed in the Art Gallery, which opened in 1917 and bears his name. Since 1917, the collection has been added to and now comprises some 10,000 items. Alongside the paintings are ceramics, textiles and some beautiful examples of Sowerby glassware.

Gateshead Municipal Council acquired Saltwell Towers in 1932 and for many years the building served as a museum of industrial and social history. In time, this multi-turreted Victorian pile sadly fell into an undignified state of disrepair and was eventually closed down. In 2002, however, Gateshead Council began a programme of refurbishment that has fully restored Saltwell Towers to its former magnificence. Locally known as the 'People's Park', the estate covers some fifty-five acres of landscape, with ornamental and woodland gardens, a boating lake, sports' facilities, bowling greens, play areas, animal house, maze, education centre and, of course, the now beautifully-restored Victorian house.

A vivid slice of life from nineteenth-century Tyneside can be experienced at the award-winning Beamish Museum, an open-air museum which was first

Postcard depicting War Memorial and Shipley Art Gallery, Gateshead. (© Gateshead Libraries.)

WAR MEMORIAL AND SHIPLEY ART GALLERY. GATESHEAD

established in 1970 on an extensive site at Beamish, to the south-west of Gateshead. Beamish is a living, working museum, whose guiding principle is to preserve examples of everyday life in the urban and rural North-East, at the climax of industrialisation in the early twentieth century. Among its many attractions on some 300 acres, it preserves a colliery, a farm and its own railway station where visitors can travel on a steam locomotive, or maybe catch a ride on an original Gateshead tram. The museum is also home to a row of terraced dwelling houses and shops that reflect domestic life at the turn of the century and contain many genuine artefacts from the period. These buildings, which originally stood at Ravensworth Terrace in Gateshead, were saved from demolition, carefully dismantled and painstakingly reassembled at Beamish.

Gateshead Tram Car 10 at the Low Fell Terminus outside S. McKinney's shop. The tram has been restored to working order and now carries passengers at Beamish Open Air Museum. (© Newcastle Libraries.)

10
WARS
AND RECESSION

The twentieth century was barely underway when in 1902, work commenced on another railway bridge across the Tyne. At the turn of the century, northbound trains on the main east-coast line were obliged to enter Newcastle's Central Station and then reverse back out in order to continue their journey, because of its layout. As the volume of rail traffic increased, this caused all kinds of problems and a decision was taken to construct the King Edward VII Rail Bridge. Built to the west of the High Level and Swing Bridges, this new bridge carried four lines that bypassed the Central Station and was completed in 1906. In July of that year, the bridge was officially opened by King Edward VII and Queen Alexandra.

Newcastle was now the financial and social hub of a prosperous and rapidly developing region with an ever-expanding population. Cars, vans and electric trams now cruised the city's busy streets and the architectural face of the city continued to develop. By 1904, the exuberant free-style façade of Emerson Chambers, designed by Benjamin Simpson and one of the finest examples of Art Nouveau architecture in the North-East, graced the area north of Grey's Monument, while in the same year, the impressive Baroque tower of the Laing Art Gallery received its finishing touches.

The 'King's Cross to Newcastle Non-Stop' crossing the King Edward VII Rail Bridge. (© Gateshead Libraries.)

The Laing Art Gallery opened in 1904 without an art collection. (Photo: Ian Scott.)

In the early years of the twentieth century, Newcastle had been remarkably deficient in venues for the display of the visual arts. Unlike Liverpool, Manchester, Sheffield and Leeds which all possessed art galleries by this time, Newcastle was almost unique in possessing no civic art gallery at all. However, the wine and spirit merchant Alexander Laing (1828-1905) finally resolved this problem by donating £20,000 to the city for civic improvements, in gratitude for the fifty years of commercial prosperity the city had afforded him. The mayor of the day directed this sum towards an art gallery subscription fund, a site was selected next to the Free Library on Bridge Street and the architects Cackett and Burns Dick were commissioned to draw up plans. The Laing Art Gallery was begun in 1901 and the Baroque tower, with its open octagonal lantern and bas-relief of female figures, was finally finished and the gallery opened to the public on 13 October 1904.

Now, Laing was not an art connoisseur or collector and the gallery was opened without a collection, causing the first curator to joke that he feared having to resort to exhibiting the wood shavings left by the carpenters for the opening exhibition! However, his fears were unfounded and the special inaugural exhibition, comprising newly-commissioned works, loans from local art collectors and national institutions, was a celebrated triumph. Building on the success of this exhibition, the City Council then decided to build up a permanent fine art collection along similar lines. The gallery also benefited from a large number of important gifts and bequests of oil paintings and watercolours from prominent local industrialists, public figures and the Contemporary Art Society, thus laying the foundations of an outstanding collection of fine arts.

For Tyneside's working population, the latter part of the Victorian Age had brought with it unprecedented changes to their lives. Medical care, education and housing had improved to an extent that would have astonished previous generations, although Tyneside slums were still amongst the worst in the land and a yawning gap remained between rich and poor.

In the build up to the First World War, the arms race intensified and Tyneside's heavy industries positively boomed. Shipyards, foundries and factories worked around the clock, churning out steel, iron, guns, munitions, tanks, warplanes, battleships, cruisers and all the deadly trappings of war. Virtually all of Tyneside's heavy industries supported one another and were at some point in their process dependent on coal fuel. For all concerned, these were prosperous times and it must have been difficult to foresee the potential danger of a local economy that was so critically dependent on so few interlocking industries.

In the early days of the war, support for 'King and Country' was deeply ingrained. Believing that the war would be over in a matter of weeks or months, optimistic crowds of men enlisted with their pals in Tyneside's proud battalions and marched off to fight the Hun. As in the rest of the country, women took over many jobs in areas that hitherto had been exclusively male-dominated and although some discovered a new kind of independence whilst supporting the war effort, their enthusiasm was inevitably dampened by ominously rising casualty lists and the dreaded prospect of a knock on the door signalling tragic news of a husband, son or father.

Thousands of Tyneside men serving in the Northumberland Fusiliers and the

'The Response', a World War 1 Memorial at Barras Bridge, is considered to be one of the finest of its kind in the country and is a Grade II listed building. Sir William Goscombe John's detailed bronze sculpture (1923) shows the 5th Northumberland Fusiliers marching down the Great North Road to the Central Station in 1915, with their families alongside. (Photo: Keith Durham.)

Durham Light Infantry were destined never to return and when hostilities ended, those that did survive came back to a home front that was already in a depressed state of economic decline. For many of them, Tyneside would be far removed from the 'land fit for heroes' that they had been so rashly promised by Lloyd George's government.

The end of the war marked an immediate decline in government orders for warships and overseas trading unexpectedly slowed down. Exports began to dwindle, coal prices dropped dramatically and by 1923, the knock-on effect had spread significantly to Tyneside's supporting industries, causing heavy unemployment across the region. At the time of the General Strike in 1926, unemployment in some areas of the North-East was running as high as 40% to 50%, and for many on Tyneside, this was a period of great hardship that would drag on into the Depression of the early 1930s.

The shipbuilding industry in particular went into serious decline. In times of hardship, ship-repair work had always proved a mainstay on Tyneside, and now many yards were relying solely on repair contracts to stay open. Due to the severe shortage of work, Armstrong Whitworth began to manufacture for the civilian market and in spite of a merger with the midlands-based firm of Vickers in 1927, the Walker Naval Yard was forced into closure the following year.

However, on Tyneside the impact of the recession was felt more in some areas than in others. By and large, most of the region's administrative, retail and service-based industries managed to emerge from the period relatively unscathed. By 1923, over 275,000 people lived in Newcastle and the increasing road traffic across the High Level and Swing Bridges was beginning to cause serious congestion. In 1925, the city was feeling affluent enough to start building a fifth bridge across the river. Designed by the engineering firm of Mott, Hay and Anderson, (who also designed the Forth Road and Sydney Harbour Bridges), and built by the Middlesbrough firm of Dorman Long, the new, green, through-arch Tyne Bridge was destined to become Tyneside's most enduring icon and was the largest single-span bridge in Britain at the time of its opening.

A generous government grant helped finance the project and in August 1925, construction teams based at Gateshead and Newcastle commenced working towards each other. These men operated in an environment that would horrify health and safety experts today. Flickering black-and-white newsreel footage has captured images of cloth-capped workmen swarming among a maze of narrow, exposed girders that jut out a hundred feet above the river. Working without safety harnesses and displaying an almost suicidal disdain for the gaping void below, these Chaplinesque figures repeatedly performed stomach-churning balancing acts that can make the viewer giddy even now.

On 25 February 1928 the two work forces met in the middle and shook

View from the Newcastle Quayside of the Tyne Bridge under construction in 1927. (© Gateshead Libraries.)

hands above the centre of the river, and in the October of that year, King George V officially opened the New Tyne Road Bridge. The construction of the bridge consumed 7,000 tons of steel and the massive 162 metre-span, which rises to a total height of 59 metres above the river, is supported on two tall towers built of Cornish granite. The towers were designed as warehouses with five storeys each, but the inner floors were never completed and as a result, the storage areas have never been used. Lifts to provide access to the Quayside for passengers and goods were built in the towers but these are no longer in use today.

The Tyne Bridge now carried the busy A1 trunk road northwards through the centre of Newcastle and this encouraged further development on Market Street and Northumberland Street. Pilgrim Street also benefited and by 1933, could boast new magistrates' courts, a police station, a fire station and a plush, state-of-the-art cinema called the Paramount. The new Tyne Bridge eased the load on the High Level Bridge and also enabled road traffic to avoid the regular delays experienced whilst attempting to cross the Swing Bridge, which at that time opened for shipping some twenty or thirty times a day.

However, the shipbuilding industry continued on its downward spiral. By 1933, the region had seen another twenty-five shipyards close down, making thousands more men unemployed. The fate of Jarrow epitomised this lamentable state of affairs. In the boom-time prior to the First World War, Palmer's Shipyard thrived and the town's population increased to around 40,000 people. In many cases, whole families were dependent on Palmer's for their living and the yard's

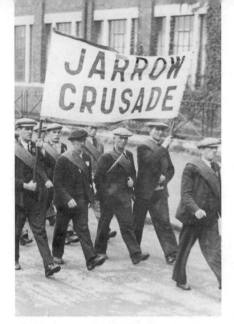

Marchers on the Jarrow Crusade, 1936.
(Photo: With kind permission of *South Shields Gazette*.)

The Paramount Cinema on Pilgrim Street, Newcastle. The flags and bunting are to celebrate the Silver Jubilee of King George V and Queen Mary in 1935. The Paramount is showing the film *The Gay Divorcee*, starring Fred Astaire and Ginger Rogers.
(© Newcastle Libraries.)

closure in 1933 resulted in Jarrow's unemployment figures reaching a staggering 70%.

In October 1936, this desperate situation resulted in the Jarrow Crusade, when two hundred unemployed men, led by a mouth-organ band and their fiery MP, Ellen Wilkinson, popularly known as 'Red Ellen', marched almost three hundred miles to the Palace of Westminster in London in an attempt to bring their plight directly to the government's attention. The marchers carried a petition, signed by 11,000 Jarrow residents, which appealed for some form of alternative employment to be founded in the town. It was duly delivered to the House of Commons, but sadly, generated little response from the government of the day. The town's shipbuilding industry remained closed and the marchers were given one pound each for the train fare back to Jarrow. Nevertheless, the Jarrow Crusade was carried out with a restrained dignity that touched the nation and will always remain deeply enshrined in Tyneside's heritage.

In that same year, the government did offer the region some small relief in the shape of the Team Valley Trading Estate at Gateshead. Having acknowledged the dangers of too much dependency on far too few heavy industries, this new industrial estate, the first initiative of its kind, was conceived in a bid to encourage the founding of smaller, lighter industries, which it was hoped, would lead the region into new areas of diversity.

It is worth emphasising that not ev-

Work started in the late 1930s, on the building of the Team Valley Trading Estate, Gateshead. (© Gateshead Libraries.)

eryone suffered during this period and the mid-1930s saw many of the region's middle classes beginning to move on to the comfortable, semi-detached housing estates which were being built in Tyneside's ever-growing suburbs on all sides. The thirties also heralded new programmes of council housing and, for around 20,000 of Tyneside's less wealthy citizens, standards of living significantly improved.

By 1938, however, Adolf Hitler had ranted, raved and pounded his fists to such an extent that once again the clouds of war began to darken Europe's horizon. Shipyards and armament factories were hurriedly re-opened, Tyneside's heavy industry quickly moved back into top gear and for a while the spectre of high unemployment seemed to disappear. At the outbreak of war in 1939, many thousands of Tyneside's men were soon absorbed into the armed services, and once again women stepped into the breach and took over many of their menfolks' tasks. Air raid wardens were appointed, sirens were tested, children were evacuated to the countryside, the blackout came into force and rationing commenced. Barrage balloons soon floated over Tyneside, large-calibre guns and machine-gun nests guarded the mouth of the River Tyne and the Home Guard was established. Pillboxes were erected at hundreds of strategic locations, while anti-aircraft batteries and searchlights swept the skies.

Throughout the war years, Tyneside's shipyards were engaged in building and repairing large numbers of merchant ships, tankers and landing craft, but warships still took pride of place. In 1939, the Walker Naval Yard built the aircraft carrier HMS *Victorious* and also launched one of her most famous battleships, HMS *King George V*. In May 1941, both these ships played a major role in the chase and destruction of the German battleship *Bismarck*. Other warships of note launched from the Walker Yard included the destroyers HMS *Hero*, HMS

BRITAIN'S SUPER BATTLESHIP H.M.S. KING GEORGE V.

Postcard of 'Britain's super battleship HMS *King George V.*' (© Newcastle Libraries.)

Hereward and HMS *Cossack*. In February 1940, whilst patrolling in Norwegian waters, it was the crew of HMS *Cossack* that liberated three hundred allied prisoners held on board the Nazi prison ship *Altmark*. Some of the imprisoned men were merchant seamen from Tyneside and all were returned safe and well to their homes and families.

Before the commencement of hostilities, the German *Luftwaffe* had already made numerous reconnaissance flights over the region and Tyneside's docks, shipyards and industrial installations were obvious targets. In July 1940, the Spillers' factory near the Keep received a direct hit when a German bomb narrowly missed the High Level Bridge, and shortly afterwards over twenty high explosive bombs fell on the city, causing casualties and widespread damage. In August 1940, some three hundred Heinkel and Junkers bombers appeared over Tyneside on a daylight raid and were duly intercepted by fighter squadrons based across the region. In the ensuing dogfight, the *Luftwaffe* suffered heavy losses and was sent packing. In 1941, Redhead's yards at West Docks in South Shields were bombed and partially wrecked and in the same year, the *Luftwaffe* targeted the Walker Yard, but luckily, only caused minor casualties and relatively little damage.

On 1 September 1941, however, in a night raid the German *Luftwaffe* dropped over 100 bombs, inflicting serious damage on Jesmond, Byker, St Peter's, Walker and Newcastle's New Bridge Street Goods Station, fires which burned for well over twenty-four hours. But when compared with the casualties experienced by other British cities that were subjected to the full wrath of the *Luftwaffe*, Newcastle's civilian population would appear to have escaped quite lightly. By and large, German air raids were concentrated further downriver and the towns of North Shields and South Shields suffered significant casualties as result of regular bombing, which caused varying degrees of damage and disrupted that region until 1943. Thousands of people were made homeless after these air raids and the ensuing fire damage, and the civil authorities spent many days cleaning up the resultant debris.

The mood of those times is beautifully captured by local author, Robert Westall, in his book *The Machine Gunners*, first published by Macmillan in 1975. The story follows the adventures of a group of lads who salvage a powerful machine-gun from a crashed German bomber and hide it in order to 'do their bit' in the event of a German invasion. The indomitable nature of Tyneside is represented by a defiant old lady, who, on the imminent threat of being overrun by German paratroopers, refuses point blank to evacuate her home. Needless to say, the 'invasion' proves to be a false alarm.

In May 1945, Germany's surrender was celebrated on Tyneside with an eruption of street parties, victory teas, victory parades and bonfires. Later that year, the war was finally ended when Japan was bombed into submission and a second round of celebrations ensued. By 1946, the people of Tyneside were ready to turn their backs on the austerity of the war years and looked forward with enthusiasm to a brighter, more vibrant future.

Unfortunately, the recovery they so much deserved was slow to come about. As far back as 1944, the imminent defeat of Nazi Germany had already prompted the government to cut back severely on the number of orders placed with Tyneside shipyards for warships and a considerable number of contracts were actually cancelled. Nevertheless, there was still a demand for passenger liners, cargo ships and oil tankers and the region's reputation for delivering soundly-built vessels meant that most of Tyneside's yards could still manage to fill their order books. By the 1960s, however, the future of Tyneside's shipbuilding industry would come under serious threat from fierce competition that was beginning to emerge, ironically enough, in Germany and Japan.

Rationing continued until 1946, and for many the immediate post-war years on Tyneside were a somewhat disappointing and cheerless period. As the 1940s dragged to a close the coal industry was nationalised, and in 1948 the National Health Service was founded. As the 1950s began to gather pace, however, the people of the North-East gradually began to enjoy their share of the nation's growing prosperity. Unemployment reached an all time low, salaries increased and a greater percentage of the population was able to afford to buy their own homes. People also had more leisure time and car ownership became more commonplace. Tyneside's workforce continued to grow.

The 24 July 1951 saw the completion of the long-awaited Tyne Pedestrian

Tyne Pedestrian and Cycle Tunnel runs under the Tyne between Howden and Jarrow. Now part of the National Cycle Network. (Photo: Graeme Peacock.)

and Cycle Tunnel, running under the river between Howden and Jarrow. When it was first opened, over a thousand people used it every day to commute to work and in recent times the numbers are slowly rising again. Today, it is an important link in the National Cycle Network, between NCN14 and NCN72. The Toll Tunnel, the third part of this Tunnel project was now under construction and eagerly awaited by Tynesiders but would not open until 1967. In that same year of 1951, one of the first of Newcastle's Chinese restaurants, the May Kway opened on Northumberland Street.

The 1950s were also a golden era for Newcastle United Football Club. Fielding such hallowed names as Joe Harvey, George Robledo and 'Wor Jackie' Milburn, the club won the Football Association Cup in 1951 and repeated this success in 1952. Tynesiders and the 'Toon Army' were ecstatic! Not content with that stunning achievement, team captain Jimmy Scoular led the club to victory in 1955 and once again a triumphant Newcastle United carried the much-prized FA Cup back to Tyneside.

Postcard of Newcastle United's AFC Cup finalists, 1951-52. (© Newcastle Libraries.)

NEWCASTLE UNITED A.F.C. CUP FINALISTS, 1951-52
R. Cowell, J. Harvey (Capt.), R. Simpson, F. Brennan, A. McMichael, E. Robledo,
T. Walker, W. Foulkes, J. Milburn, G. Robledo, R. Mitchell.

11
THE SIXTIES AND BEYOND

The next two decades would see monumental changes to the face of Tyneside and to Newcastle, in particular. The 1960s saw the region enjoying an even higher standard of living in a relaxed era of pop culture, permissiveness, bingo halls, nightclubs and pub meals – of course, everyone had to try scampi in a basket and Black Forest Gateau! In Newcastle, Tynesiders frequented trendy nightspots such as the Dolce Vita, Grey's Club, the Cavendish and the Club-A-Go-Go. The city's dance halls were popular venues for both sexes and many a tryst was arranged at the Mayfair Ballroom on Newgate Street (site of the present Gate leisure complex), the Oxford Dancehall in New Bridge Street (now a nightclub) and the legendary Majestic Ballroom on Westgate Road (now home to the Carling Academy).

As the Beatles took the world by storm, Tyneside's own pop group, The Animals, launched their unique rendering of the blue's classic, 'House of the Rising Sun', which rocketed up the charts and became forever linked with images of Tyneside. The 1960s were also boom times for the North-East's Working Men's Clubs and Institute Unions, popularly known as the CIU clubs, which were affluent enough to host top class artists such as Tom Jones and Shirley Bassey. Audiences also flocked to these clubs to see Tyneside's favourite comedian, Bobby Thompson, nicknamed 'The Little Waster', whose wry observations on life amongst Tyneside's working classes still make audiences howl with laughter today.

Newcastle United entered the 1960s relegated to the Second Division, but in 1964, former team captain Joe Harvey was appointed as manager and stayed for thirteen years. By the 1964-65

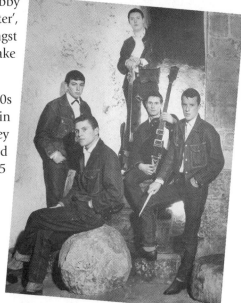

Publicity shot of Eric Burdon and The Animals, taken at Newcastle's Castle Keep; left to right: Eric Burdon (Vocals) Alan Price (Keyboards) Chas Chandler (Bass) Hliton Valentine (Guitar) John Steel (Drums). (Photo: Commons Library Wikipedia.)

season, Harvey was fielding a dynamic range of players that included Ron McGarry, Bob Moncur and Alan Suddick, and by the end of that season, Newcastle was back in the First Division once again.

Road traffic across the region continued to increase and in order to alleviate some of the growing congestion on Tyneside's bridges, the long-awaited Tyne Road Tunnel was opened by Queen Elizabeth II on 19 October 1967 at a cost of £12.5 million, but actually only commenced operational use in 1968 when the northern link roads were completed. It was built on more or less the same lines as the first Pedestrian Tunnel, being 1,700 metres long with a diameter of 9.5 metres, and a roadbed of 7.3 metres. Designed to carry about 25,000 vehicles a day, this was soon increased to a traffic build-up of around 36,000 vehicles a day. Amazingly, the original toll for cars using this tunnel was two shillings and six pence, the equivalent nowadays is 12.5 pence!

To the west of Newcastle, 1967 also saw the opening of the Scotswood Road Bridge, designed by Mott, Hay and Anderson and built by Mitchell Construction and Dorman Long. This bridge replaced the old Scotswood Bridge built in 1831, locally known as the 'Chain Bridge', and was built slightly to the west of it. It is a box-girder bridge, supported by two piers in the river and carries a dual carriageway road.

All was not rosy, however, and due to increasing competition from around the world, Tyneside's shipping industry seriously began to contract. In 1968, Swan Hunter was forced into a merger with the remaining shipyards on the river and

A 1966 view of the Scotswood Bridges taken from Heath Crescent, Newcastle-upon-Tyne. On the right is the second Scotswood Bridge which is under construction. On the left is the first Scotswood Bridge which is still being used by traffic. The second Scotswood Bridge was not completed until 1967.
(© Bridges Collection: Newcastle Libraries.)

Towering over the terraced streets of Wallsend, *Esso Northumbria* at Swan Hunter Wallsend 1969.
(© Ships' Collection: Newcastle Libraries.)

took the name Swan Hunter and Tyne Shipbuilders , which, after a further merger with the Furness Yard in 1969 became Swan Hunter Shipbuilders. A lifeline for the industry came in 1969, when Swan Hunter's Wallsend Yard launched the super tanker *Esso Northumbria*. This gigantic, crude carriership was the largest of its kind to have been built in Britain in 1969 and the first of eight similar vessels that the yard would subsequently construct.

Back in the city, work progressed throughout the 1960s on a bold, new Civic Centre, which would bring all the city's services under one roof. Designed by the city's architect George Kenyon, it was completed in 1967 and formally opened by King Olav V of Norway on 14 November 1968. Newcastle's Civic Centre is universally applauded as one of the city's finest new buildings. The Centre's lofty tower is constructed from white Portland stone and is crowned with a turret of thin vertical fins decorated with seahorses' heads, and high above, the three golden castles of the city's coat of arms; also incorporated is a carillon containing twenty-five bells, which rings out a medley of local tunes at specific times. At the head of the Ceremonial Way and looming over the main entrance to the Civic Centre is David Wynne's impressive 'Tyne River God' fountain. Cast in bronze and weighing over two tonnes, this giant figure portrays the river god in human form, a fountain within his outstretched hand courses a constant stream of water along the length of this aquatic deity.

12
UPS AND DOWNS

Unfortunately, this vibrant era was marred by the activities of one of its leading and most dynamic figures. In 1960, when T. Dan Smith was elected as the leader of Newcastle City Council, he set about launching a sweeping programme of slum clearances and compulsory purchase orders that were designed to create space for his grandiose vision of a civic regeneration that would turn Newcastle into a renaissance city, his envisioned 'Brasilia of the North'.

Smith's modernising plans included a new polytechnical college, new road systems, urban motorways, high profile architecture and a massive indoor shopping complex that was to be situated at the centre of the city and would alter the appearance of Newcastle forever. Smith, who became known as 'Mr Newcastle', was appointed chairman of the Northern Economic Planning Council and his sphere of influence broadened accordingly. In his labyrinthine dealings, he became financially involved with the architect John Poulson and a Durham county councillor named Andrew Cunningham. In 1974, charges of corruption were brought against all three men and Smith's promising career ended in ignominy when he and his two associates were sent to jail.

Inevitably, the scandal tarnished Newcastle's reputation and the city's civic pride took many years to recover from the experience. The era of the 1960s was featured in the excellent 1996 BBC television drama *Our Friends in the North*, in which actor Alun Armstrong gave a bravura performance as Austin Donohue, a character based on the charismatic T. Dan Smith.

Many of Newcastle's older, established buildings fell victim to Smith's grandiose vision of Brutalist architecture. In order to accommodate the new Eldon Square shopping complex, most of John Dobson's elegant, terraced houses at old Eldon Square were demolished. This was perceived by Tyneside traditionalists as an act of wanton destruction and typified some of the less palatable aspects of the sixties' redevelopments. Among Smith's other Brutalist legacies were Eldon Square, Newcastle Polytechnic (later to become the University of Northumbria), the City Library and the Swan House office block, which sadly displaced Newcastle's elegant Royal Arcade.

The Royal Arcade, which had been designed by John Dobson in 1832, was carefully dismantled and at the time, it was proposed to erect the structure elsewhere, but the initiative faded and the stonework now lies buried on a site at Shieldfield to the east of the city centre. Of all the office blocks that began to appear across the region in the 1960s, one of the least appealing was Westgate House, a 46-metre (150 feet) office block, which jutted out obtrusively on concrete stilts into an otherwise pleasing area at the junction of Westgate Road and Collingwood Street, just opposite Newcastle's Central Station. It was without doubt one of Newcastle's most loathed buildings and no tears were shed at its demolition in early 2007 by its owners, the now defunct regional development agency, One North East. However, its neighbour, Norwich Union House still remains and its redevelopment has yet to be taken forward.

Another part of T. Dan Smith's grand plan for the city was to clear the slums and build decent housing. However, his high-rise housing plans were some of the most bitterly criticised in later years, destroying as they did closely-knit communities, particularly in the Scotswood Road and Elswick areas. The ten tower blocks at Cruddas Park, built by Wimpey to a Swedish modular design, were named after George Cruddas, a director of the Armstrong armament works lining the nearby northern bank of the Tyne. These blocks replaced a small park and a community of terraced housing and were named after trees and bushes such as The Sycamores, The Willows, The Poplars and King's Meadows. They were to become part of the city's skyline for over fifty years and a monument to T. Dan

View of the controversial high rise flats in Cruddas Park, Elswick taken in 1965. New residents were reassured by the modern facilities offered including: 'kitchens with electric cookers and washboilers, with tiles around the working areas and above the stainless steel sinks.' (© Newcastle Libraries.)

Get Carter multi-storey car park designed by Rodney Gordon opened in 1967 as part of the Trinity Square shopping complex in Gateshead. It was demolished in 2010. (© Newcastle Libraries.)

Smith's vision of a 'city in the sky' to replace slum terraces.

Another example of what has become known as Smith's Brutalist architecture was the multi-storey car park in Gateshead opened in 1967 and popularly known as the *Get Carter* Carpark, because of its prominent role in the 1971 film *Get Carter*. It had seven tiers of parking decks, raised above the adjoining shopping centre by a forest of support columns. The car park was commissioned as part of the redevelopment of the market square in Gateshead town centre, but the landscaping created an exposed and unattractive shopping precinct on two levels with very poor access. The rooftop café remained empty and never found a tenant.

This car park served as the location for several key scenes in what is arguably Britain's best ever gangster movie, *Get Carter*, in which Michael Caine played Jack Carter, a gangster based in London, who returns home to Tyneside to investigate the suspicious circumstances surrounding his brother's death. In the film, corrupt local businessman Cliff Brumby (Bryan Mosley) gives Jack Carter a tour of the incomplete rooftop café, saying that he is in the process of making it into a restaurant. The car park can be seen in the distance of a variety of gritty locations in and around Gateshead and Newcastle. Since the film's release in 1971, it has deservedly achieved cult status and as an added bonus, provides us with a unique and colourful snapshot of Tyneside in the sixties.

When the new Civic Centre was formally opened in 1968, Newcastle's old Town Hall in the Bigg Market, which had been used to house a variety of exhibitions and had become increasingly dilapidated, was subsequently demolished in 1969. That same year, Neil Armstrong (who could trace his lineage back to the Anglo-Scottish Border country) took a giant step for mankind on the moon, and in Newcastle construction work began on the long-planned Eldon Square Shopping Centre. Newcastle United managed to end the decade with a flourish when its football team, strengthened by Wyn Davies and Bryan Robson, won the Inter-Cities Fairs Cup in 1969.

13
TYNESIDE IN THE SEVENTIES

Many of the city council's plans from the 1960s were not initiated until the following decade and throughout the seventies Newcastle's skyline seemed forever dominated by towering cranes. The town centre, which came to resemble a giant building site, was in a constant state of upheaval and irritated motorists were plagued by an endless series of traffic diversions. Outlying areas did not escape the bulldozers either and large areas of terraced housing on both sides of the river fell prey to ambitious slum clearance orders. Cobbled streets, corner shops and favourite pubs all disappeared, and with varying degrees of consultation, whole communities were decanted into high-rise flats and newly-built council estates. For many of Tyneside's population this era marked the beginning of a bright new way of life. For others, however, the sweeping changes were a mixed blessing and many lamented the passing of traditional Tyneside life and all it stood for.

These unsettling and far-reaching social changes became the subject of one of the BBC's most successful comedy series, *The Likely Lads*, which was followed by *Whatever happened to the Likely Lads?* Both series, written by local writer, Ian La Frenais and his associate Dick Clement, centred on the everyday lives of two friends, Terry Collier and Bob Ferris, played respectively by James Bolam and Rodney Bewes. The character of Bob Ferris typified all that was new and upcoming on Tyneside, including a good job, a fiancée, his own car and the prospect of a smart new 'semi' on the fictitious Elm Lodge Estate. Terry Collier, however, bewildered by the changes taking place around him, clung to his Geordie roots and hankered for how things used to be. Later on, in the seventies, James Bolam took the lead role in the period drama *When the Boat Comes In*, a critically

Dominating the skyline, Derwent Tower (also known as the 'Dunston Rocket') was a 29-storey residential apartment building in Dunston. Work started in February 1968, and completed in March 1971 only to be demolished in 2012.
(© Gateshead Council.)

71

acclaimed series that followed the fortunes of Jack Ford, a soldier who returns to Tyneside after service in the First World War.

The seventies proved to be a period of rising unemployment on Tyneside and some of its workforce migrated south and even further afield in their search for work. This situation led the writing team of La Frenais and Clement to pen the enormously successful *Auf Wiedersehen, Pet,* which featured the adventures of a group of displaced Geordie 'brickies' working abroad in Düsseldorf. Once again, two distinct Tyneside types were highlighted in the characters of Neville, a homesick, decent family man played by Kevin Whately and the more traditional Geordie rogue in the shape of Oz, played by Tyneside actor, singer and writer, Jimmy Nail.

Numerous sequels followed and Nail went on to star in the TV dramas *Spender* and *Crocodile Shoes,* both of which featured extensive Tyneside locations. Another big favourite was the children's series *Byker Grove.* This long-running series was a springboard for Anthony McPartlin and Declan Donnelly, otherwise known as Ant and Dec, who went on to host their own show, *Ant and Dec's Saturday Night Takeaway* and are now two of the country's top paid, celebrity performers.

In Gateshead, the town's new Western Bypass was completed in the early seventies. This road system carried a dual carriageway that diverted much north and south bound traffic away from the town's centre and helped alleviate the traffic jams which still regularly occurred on the Tyne and High Level Bridges. The new road crossed the Tyne over the Scotswood Road Bridge.

Construction work inside a Metro tunnel, Newcastle-upon-Tyne taken in 1977. The photograph shows men working inside the tunnel. (© Transport Collection: Newcastle Libraries.)

Newcastle Central Motorway East was finally opened in 1975. (Photo: Ian Scott.)

In May 1971 Newcastle United was busy signing up a dynamic young striker named Malcolm MacDonald for a club record transfer fee of £180,000, and in 1974, the club reached the FA Cup final. They were, however, defeated by Liverpool and at the end of the 1974-75 season, Joe Harvey resigned as manager of the club. By the mid-seventies the club's fortunes had waned and in 1978 the 'Magpies' were relegated to the Second Division. It was a dismal period for fans.

Much to the relief of commuters across the region, Newcastle's Central Motorway East was finally opened to traffic in 1975 and the following year Eldon Square Shopping Centre opened its doors to the public, most of whom agreed that it had been well worth the long wait. This massive, spacious complex currently employs thousands of people in its shops and department stores and also includes a Recreation Centre and the new Greenmarket. In 1977, before the city had time to catch its breath once more, work began on the Tyneside's Rapid Transit System – known universally as The Metro – and Newcastle and its environs were once again plunged into a turmoil of construction works and cranes.

Meanwhile, to the east of the city, builders were engaged on the construction of the famous Byker Wall, a block of six hundred and twenty maisonettes in the Byker district of Newcastle. Following partial slum clearance of pre-war, back-to-back housing in the area, Byker residents were extensively consulted before any work commenced on the colourful new development. Their views were taken on board and an attempt was made – and largely achieved – to recreate the sense of community that had so often been lost in previous council developments. The new housing block was designed by notable architect Ralph Erskine, assisted by executive architect Vernon Gracie. The Byker Wall was completed in 1981 and the scheme would appear to have worked out to everyone's satisfaction. From an architectural viewpoint, the development has been frequently cited as an example of enlightened town planning. Its functionalist, romantic styling, with textured, complex facades, colourful brick, wood and plastic panels, attention to context and relatively low-rise construction represented a break with the high-rise, Brutalist architecture prevalent at that time. Byker Wall is on UNESCO's list of outstanding twentieth-century buildings, and in January 2007 the Byker Estate, of which the Wall forms a part, was to become a grade two-star listed building.

Alas, the 1970s were destined to end in a gloomy 'winter of discontent', but on Tyneside there were at least two things to look forward to. Every year, at Newcastle's City Hall, Christmas concerts performed by top local band 'Lindisfarne' were sell-out events and performances of their own songs, 'Fog on the Tyne' and 'Run for Home', invariably brought the house down. The second thing to look forward to, for those in the know, was the latest issue of *Viz*.

Initially, Chris Donald, who created and produced the comic *Viz* in 1979 from his bedroom in his parents' house in Jesmond, began to sell copies around Newcastle's pubs with help from his brother Simon and his friend Jim Brownlow. As the comic grew in popularity, it soon became a bestseller across the region. Chris's bedroom became too small to handle production and it moved to an office nearby in Jesmond. Chris hired another freelance artist, Simon Thorp, and for over a decade these four formed the nucleus of *Viz*. Featuring the outrageous antics of characters such as 'The Two Fat Slags', 'Biffa Bacon', 'Sid the Sexist' and 'Roger Mellie, the Man on the Telly', the *Viz* comic was guaranteed to offend and went from strength to strength, eventually hitting the shelves at WH Smith's like a breath of fresh air. The comic's fame soon spread nationwide, was taken over by a series of national publishers, and *Viz* is now well-embedded in Tyneside's folklore.

The year 1979 also saw the release of *Alien*, one of the most frightening science fiction films ever to erupt on to the screen. The film, which was a box office success around the world, was the work of film director Sir Ridley Scott, who hailed from South Shields. Scott went on to direct other smash hits such as *Blade Runner*, *Thelma and Louise*, *Black Rain* and his tour de force, *Gladiator*. Not to be outdone, his talented younger brother Tony Scott, followed up with his own successes including *Top Gun* and *Crimson Tide*, before his tragic and untimely death in August 2012.

First edition of *Viz* which hit the shelves in 1979. A first edition was sold for £350. (Photo: courtesy Lew Stringer.)

Cover of Lindisfarne's 'Fog On The Tyne' album.

14

TYNESIDE IN THE EIGHTIES

When the Tyne and Wear Metro system began operation in 1980, it was the second modern railway in Britain, after Merseyrail, to make use of existing railway alignments to create a modern rail transit system, linking them with purpose-built tunnels which run under central Newcastle and Gateshead. Although described as a modern light rail system, it is in fact a hybrid, displaying elements of light rail, heavy underground metro, and longer-distance, higher speed, suburban and inter-urban railway systems. The Metro loops around Tyneside, skirting the river and passing through areas such as Wallsend, North Shields, Tynemouth, Whitley Bay, Longbenton, Gosforth, Jesmond and Newcastle city centre. In 1991, the Metro branched out to Newcastle International Airport, and to the south, the line was carried across the Tyne on the Queen Elizabeth II Bridge to Gateshead. From there, it was extended to South Shields and to Sunderland in 2002. The many years of disruption surrounding the Metro's construction are now long forgotten and every day, thousands of Tyneside's commuters have reason to be grateful for its existence. Nowadays, it would be difficult to imagine Tyneside without its Metro.

Trams started operating on the newly opening Tyne & Wear Metro system in the early 1980s. (Photo: Graeme Peacock.)

In the early years of the eighties, unemployment figures on Tyneside rose and then fell again, house prices soared and for the third time, Redheugh Bridge was replaced by a sleeker, more up-to-date model. The third incarnation of Redheugh Bridge, designed by Mott, Hay and Anderson and constructed by Edmund Nuttall Limited, is quite an improvement on its predecessors. It is much larger and wider, can carry loads of up to 4,000 tonnes and has a life expectancy of one hundred and twenty years. Only the south abutment now remains of the original crossing and this is adorned by a modern sculpture designed by Richard Deacon.

On 28 June 1981, 12,000 runners from all over Tyneside streamed across the Tyne Bridge when former Olympic 10,000-metre bronze medallist and BBC sports commentator, Brendan Foster, organised the first ever Great North Run between

Competitors crossing the Tyne Bridge in Tyneside's annual half marathon, The Great North Run, which winds its way from Newcastle to South Shields. (Photo: Graeme Peacock.)

Newcastle and South Shields. In the first year it was advertised as a local fun run, but this annual half-marathon road race has now become established as one of Tyneside's most popular events and one of the biggest running events in the world. It is now held annually in September and thousands of participants raise thousands of pounds for various charities every year.

In 1982, Newcastle United signed former England captain, Kevin Keegan and with support from such stalwarts as Chris Waddle, Terry McDermott and Peter Beardsley, Keegan soon led the team back into the First Division, playing no less than seventy-eight times and scoring forty-eight goals. Having considerably livened up Newcastle's performance, Keegan announced his retirement prior to the end of the 1983-84 season, much to the disappointment of all his fans. His contribution to ending Newcastle's six-year absence from the First Division earned him iconic status on Tyneside. A rapid succession of team managers then came and went and by the end of the decade the club was back in the Second Division again. However, this period was not all doom and gloom and on 13 April 1985, a young Gateshead lad named Paul Gascoigne played his first game for United at St James' Park against Queen's Park Rangers, coming on as a substitute. He made a total of ninety-two appearances for Newcastle United, scoring twenty-one goals, before moving on to Tottenham Hotspur three years later for a record fee of £2 million. Following an erratic football career punctuated with flashes of pure brilliance, 'Gazza' has become well-established as a Geordie icon.

During the 1980s, the coal industry contracted dramatically and this

Type 22 frigate, HMS *Chatham*, the last warship to be built on the Tyne at the Neptune Yard, Wallsend. (Photo: POA(Phot) Owen King/MOD.)

industrial unrest culminated in the Great Miners' Strike of 1984. By the end of this decade, only a handful of working collieries would manage to survive in the region. The shipbuilding industry also began to shrink again and although the aircraft carrier HMS *Illustrious* was launched in 1978 and the flagship of the Royal Navy, HMS *Ark Royal* was launched in 1985 by Swan Hunter's Wallsend Yard, the Walker Naval Shipyard shut down in 1986, and HMS *Chatham* proved to be the last ship built at the Neptune Yard, which closed down in 1988.

Newcastle's first opportunity to host the Cutty Sark Tall Ships' Race, forerunner of the Tall Ships' Races, came in 1986 and large crowds of spectators, including Queen Elizabeth II, thronged the riverbanks to watch the stately flotilla of tall-masted vessels enter the River Tyne. These magnificent ships and their crews

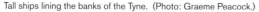

Tall ships lining the banks of the Tyne. (Photo: Graeme Peacock.)

Sir John Hall's brainchild, the Metro Centre indoor-shopping centre opened in 1986. (Photo: Graeme Peacock.).

were given a rapturous welcome on Tyneside and Newcastle's Quayside positively buzzed with excitement for the duration of their stay.

A massive boost for Tyneside came in April of the same year with the opening of the first phase of the Metro Centre, a huge, indoor-shopping complex, built on a site to the west of Gateshead, just off the Western Bypass. The complex was the brainchild of entrepreneur Sir John Hall and its construction was financed by the Church Commissioners of England. The industrial site on which it is built was purchased for a mere £100,000 back in the early seventies. and it now contains hundreds of shops, numerous restaurants, department stores and a multi-screen cinema. Employing a large number of local people, the development has steadily expanded and continues to do so with retail and leisure floor space occupying some 194,4000 square metres, with additional retail space available in the adjoining Metro Retail Park. Easily accessible by road or rail, the Metro Centre, now called 'intu Metro Centre', also offers free parking for thousands of cars and its continuing success can be measured by the fact that, on occasion, parking spaces are extremely difficult, if not impossible to find.

Eldon Square's indoor-shopping complex was not to be outdone and in 1989, this was extended over Percy Street to create Eldon Square Gardens. This year also marked the demise of Lord Armstrong's old Elswick Works and Yard, which were finally demolished and replaced by the Newcastle Business Park. By the early 1990s the Business Park, which specialised in information technology, was employing almost 4,000 local people. Armstrong, that grand old Victorian entrepreneur, would have had no quarrel with that!

15
NEWCASTLE IN THE NINETIES

In 1990, Newcastle's Western Bypass opened and the Blaydon Road Bridge, linking it to Gateshead's established Western Bypass, carried the A1 across the Tyne. This massive undertaking has proved to be a significant step towards cutting down the traffic congestion on Tyneside.

Regeneration on Newcastle's Quayside was also gathering pace and by 1990, the colossal red sandstone pillars of the new Law Courts dominated the area around Broad Chare. Built by the local architectural practice of Napper Collerton, using red sandstone from Dumfriesshire, it was one of the first new developments in a plan for the rejuvenation of a redundant and run-down dock area beside the River Tyne. Within a year, the prestigious Copthorne Hotel graced Newcastle's waterfront on a site opposite the remains of the town wall in the Close. In the city centre, a new four-storey shopping arcade named the Monument Mall was completed. Situated just to the north of Grey's Monument and adjacent to the Monument metro station, this tastefully designed development blends seamlessly

Newcastle's Western Bypass and Gateshead's Western Bypass were finally linked in 1990 by the Blaydon Road Bridge. (Photo: Ian Scott.)

Brainchild of ex-Animals' member Chas Chandler and Nigel Stanger, the Metro Arena has become the largest indoor concert hall and exhibition centre in the North-East of England. (Photo: Ian Scott.)

into its classical surroundings and is home to a variety of national and independent retailers.

In 1992, Newcastle gained a new university as Newcastle Polytechnic was officially inaugurated as the University of Northumbria at Newcastle. It had its origins in three regional colleges: Rutherford College of Technology, the College of Art and Industrial Design and the Municipal College of Commerce, all of which were amalgamated to form Newcastle Polytechnic in 1969. It later became the major regional centre for training teachers, when it incorporated the City College of Education in 1974 and the Northern Counties College of Education in 1976. To the great delight of Tynesiders, Newcastle Poly was part of the UK-wide process in 1992, in which polytechnics were redesignated as new universities, giving the city two universities they could take pride in.

In February 1992, almost eight years after his final game as a player, Kevin Keegan was lured out of retirement and came back to St James' Park, this time as club manager of Newcastle United. At the same time, Sir John Hall took over the running of the club and financed the rebuilding of St James' Park, much to the delight of the 'Toon Army', the name adopted by United's ever-loyal supporters. Once again, Keegan's presence revitalised the club and a dynamic squad, including Andy Cole, Barry Venison and Pavel Srnicek, thrilled the fans and Newcastle United stormed to victory as First Division Champions. By the 1993-94 season, local football legend Peter Beardsley was wowing the crowds and Newcastle United was firmly back in the Premier Division.

In July 1993, the Cutty Sark Tall Ships' Race from Tyneside to Bergen took place and the region again welcomed the fleet with a programme of special events, a fireworks' display, live music and plenty of liquid refreshment. Once again, the Quayside was a hub of activity as thousands of people from all over Britain admired the magnificent vessels and exchanged banter with crews from around the world. Many young Tyneside girls overcame the language barrier and became very attached to young sailors from the giant Russian and Polish training ships and when the fleet sailed out of the Tyne, there were many tearful farewells. It is worth noting that, along with some happy memories, this prestigious event is estimated to have generated over £38 million in revenue for the region.

Although Newcastle's City Hall was still a favourite venue for international performers, Tyneside became an even more attractive option with the completion of the Newcastle Arena, later known as the Telewest Arena, and then renamed the Metro Radio Arena after a new sponsorship deal was signed with local station Metro Radio. The Arena was built on the riverside, near the Redheugh Bridge and opened in November 1995. It was the brainchild of musician and ex-Animals' member Chas Chandler and his business partner Nigel Stanger, cost £10 million to build, has an audience capacity of over 11,000 and has played host to a succession of top class performers, including David Bowie, Robbie Williams, Madness, Kylie Minogue, the Corrs and local singer-songwriter Sting. The Arena also hosts basketball, championship tennis and snooker and is the largest concert hall and exhibition venue in the North-East.

In 1990, Newcastle Gosforth Rugby Club moved to its new grounds at Kingston Park which had been purchased for £55,000. Prior to this, the site had been the *Newcastle Chronicle* and *Journal* sports grounds. For the 1996-97 season the new name of Newcastle Falcons and new black-and-white colours were adopted, after local businessman Sir John Hall took control of the club. Newcastle Falcons was the first fully professional club in the world. The year 1995 saw the club earn promotion from the national second division to the premiership and in the following season Newcastle became English champions at their first attempt. Hall sold the Falcons for a nominal sum in 1999 to local businessman Dave Thompson, under whom the Falcons won two PowerGen Cups.

In 1996, Newcastle United paid £15 million for one of its most enduring stars, the now legendary striker and local hero, Alan Shearer. Having brought in an international bevy of players such as Ginola, Asprilla and Les Ferdinand, Kevin Keegan resigned from the club in January 1997. Kenny Dalglish took over his position and a year later, the club was narrowly defeated in the FA Cup Final by Arsenal. In 1999, Newcastle had yet another new manager, the former Dutch player Ruud Gullit, and once again the club reached Wembley Stadium only to be defeated by Manchester United. Gullit left the club shortly afterwards and was replaced by veteran manager Bobby Robson, who went on to save the club from relegation and has become something of a Tyneside legend in his own right.

16
GATESHEAD POINTS THE WAY

Living under the shadow of its larger, prestigious neighbour, Gateshead was often dismissed in history as little more than a back lane into Newcastle. Over the past fifty years, however, a bold and progressive Gateshead Council has dispelled that image forever. In recent times, Gateshead has gone through a breathtaking era of transformation and now spearheads the region's current programme of regeneration.

The extensive redevelopment of Gateshead International Stadium in the seventies and again in 2006 and 2010 has enabled the town to host a succession of top class events, and this strong support for athletics put Gateshead firmly on the sporting map. The stadium can hold audiences of 12,000 now and its capacity makes it the third largest stadium on Tyneside, and the sixth largest in north-east England. The main arena is principally used for athletics. The inaugural athletics competition in 1974, the 'Gateshead Games', was instigated by Brendan Foster, then a Gateshead Council employee. This began a tradition of athletics' competitions at the stadium, which has since hosted the British Grand Prix and the European Team Championships. Many of Gateshead's athletes have attained international status and runners such as Brendan Foster, Steve Cram, Mike McLeod and Jonathan Edwards still have close links with the town.

'Sports Day', the 4-metre high sculpture of reinforced, painted concrete was made on site on West Street by Mike Winstone, Gateshead's sculptor in residence from 1985-86. (Photo: Keith Durham.)

In the sixties and seventies, sweeping programmes of slum clearance, combined with sensible town planning, have resulted in attractive housing schemes across the borough and the Council's award-winning horticultural arm has enhanced Gateshead's parks and open spaces. In 1987, Gateshead Council brought the majority of its services together in an attractive new Civic Centre on Regent Street, close to the town centre. When the borough hosted the National Garden Festival in 1990, the site featured a number of intriguing pieces of modern art which paved the

Over the past decades Gateshead International Stadium has been redeveloped and updated, enabling it to be in the forefront of attracting top athletes to major athletic events. (© Gateshead Libraries.)

way for future promotion of artworks.

An important part of Gateshead's clean-up was the demolition of the *Get Carter* Carpark. In June 2007, the Council and site owners Tesco confirmed plans to demolish it. Attempts had been made in the 1990s to preserve it, mainly because of its part in the film *Get Carter*, a classic of British cinema. Even Sylvester Stallone lent his weight to the calls for its preservation as a cinematic landmark, but to no avail. A final tour of its upper levels was held in April 2008 and many Tynesiders voiced their regret at the loss of this iconic landmark from the skyline. Demolition commenced in July 2010 and Gateshead Council enterprisingly styled the remains as 'commemorative pieces of concrete', selling them off in specially decorated tins for £5 each!

Over the next decade, Gateshead Council went on to champion contemporary art by commissioning a series of ground-breaking and often controversial sculptures for display in public places. The most famous of these, without doubt, is the 'Angel of the North', which stands on a hill on the southern edge of Low Fell, overlooking the A1 and A167 roads into Tyneside and dominating the southerly approach to the town. Designed by Sir Antony Gormley OBE and erected in February 1998, this gigantic steel icon is impossible to ignore and is seen by around 33 million people each year. Towering 20 metres high with a wingspan of 54 metres across, the 'Angel' (affectionately known locally as 'The Gateshead Flasher') was crafted from 200 tonnes of steel and fabricated in Hartlepool. The wings of the 'Angel' do not stand straight sideways, but are angled 3.5 degrees forward, and Gormley did this to create a warm sense of embrace. After some early misgivings, the 'Angel' has now become an accepted and increasingly admired part of Tyneside's ever-expanding cultural heritage.

Other open-air works of art are also prominently displayed in Gateshead's town centre and in the award-winning Riverside Sculpture Park. This willingness to champion contemporary art by turning its words into action placed Gateshead in a prime position when bidding for arts-related grants and has resulted in the spectacular regeneration of its quayside area. In the mid-nineties, work began on the redundant shell of the old Baltic Flour Mills on the quayside and Baltic Centre for Contemporary Art (BALTIC) began to take shape, finally opening its doors in 2002.

However, the first major step in Gateshead's quayside regeneration, was the concept of a new bridge for pedestrians and cyclists, which would link the quay's arts quarter on the south bank up with Newcastle's Quayside area across the river. A design submitted by Wilkinson Eyre Architects and structural engineers Gifford & Partners was approved and the Gateshead-based company, Harbour and General, began work on the Millennium Bridge. What many still regard as Gateshead's crowning achievement came to fruition on a beautiful, sunny morning on 20 November 2000. In front of thousands of enraptured onlookers, the magnificent Millennium Bridge, delicately suspended from a colossal, floating crane, the *Asian Hercules II*, drifted slowly upriver. As all on Tyneside held their collective breath, the vast, slender arc was carefully lowered onto its abutments and moments later, thousands of Geordies gasped in delight at their brand new, shimmering icon.

The Bridge, which cost £22 million, part-funded by the Millennium Commission and European Regional Development Fund, was built by Volker Stevin and was the first in the world to open on a tilting mechanism, which turns on pivots secured on both sides of the riverbank. The Bridge's mechanism is operated by six 45cm-diameter, hydraulic rams, three on each side, each powered by an energy-efficient, electric motor. When it tilts to allow shipping to pass underneath, the Millennium Bridge resembles a gigantic eyelid, opening and closing, which has led to its affectionate nickname, the 'Blinking Eye Bridge'. It takes as little as five minutes to rotate through the full forty degrees from closed to open, depending on wind speed.

Since its opening, Gateshead's Millennium Bridge has attracted worldwide attention and has been showered with awards, including the prestigious RIBA Stirling Award for Best Architectural Structure. It was listed as one of Time Magazine's Best Innovations of 2001 and in 2005, the bridge received the Outstanding Structure Award from the International Association for Bridge and Structural Engineering (IABSE).

The £46 million Baltic Centre for Contemporary Art (BALTIC) opened to the public at midnight on Saturday 13 July 2002, in the shell of the Baltic Flour Mills, which had been built in 1950 by the Rank Hovis company to a late-1930s design by architects Gelder and Kitchen. BALTIC contains over 3,000 square metres of art space, housing five galleries for the display of contemporary visual art. It has hosted many temporary exhibitions by internationally-renowned contemporary artists that have intrigued and bemused the millions of visitors who have passed

Baltic Centre for Contemporary Art (BALTIC) left and behind, the luxury residential apartments, which along with Sage Gateshead, have transformed the Gateshead Quayside. (Photo: Graeme Peacock.)

through its doors. BALTIC also has a free drop-in art library with over 11,000 books, magazines, videos and films on previous BALTIC exhibitions and computer access to thousands of archive images and documents. The Centre is crowned by a restaurant with panoramic views of the cityscape. At ground level visitors can also enjoy refreshments in the BALTIC kitchen.

There can be little doubt that during these years Gateshead effectively stole a march over its larger neighbour Newcastle, across the water. When a new concert hall for the Northern Sinfonia Orchestra was being discussed in the early nineties, both Newcastle and Gateshead showed an interest in the project. While Newcastle dithered, Gateshead eagerly grasped the opportunity, secured the necessary funding primarily through National Lottery grants and the £70 million Sage Gateshead, a great, curved, glass and stainless steel building began to rise above the Gateshead Quays. Designed and built for Gateshead Council by internationally-respected architects Norman Foster & Partners, the spectacular, award-winning Sage opened to great public acclaim and fanfare on 17 December 2004. Structurally, it comprises three separate buildings, insulated from each other to prevent noise and vibration between them, with the capacity for a 1,700-seater hall, a 450-seater hall and a smaller rehearsal and performance hall. It also has five bars, a brasserie, a café and a multi-purpose function room.

Catering for all kinds of music in its concert halls and smaller performance areas, the Sage provides world-class acoustic facilities for the performance of both amateur and professional music. It is now also the permanent home of the Northern Sinfonia, of the North Music Trust and of Folkworks, the regional folk music and dance organisation. This giant, glass-fronted, futuristic development, which has become a truly stunning landmark on Tyneside's riverside frontage, can also double up as a conference centre. Shortly after it was opened, Sage Gateshead was the chosen venue for the Labour Party Conference in 2005 and more recently, the Liberal Democrat Party conference in 2012.

17
NEWCASTLE IN THE NOUGHTIES

By 1999, the vast majority of the region's pits had been closed down and Tyneside's once flourishing coal trade was no more than a distant memory, consigned to nostalgic television documentaries and a growing number of museums and heritage trails. When compared with the previous century, the region's shipbuilding industry had become virtually non-existent and its dwindling work force was almost totally reliant on ship-repair work. However, some respite has been forthcoming in the form of the offshore oil and gas industries, which have become important sources of revenue for the region and provide employment for thousands of local people all over Tyne and Wear.

Recession and recovery

The recession which hit the global economy in 2007, inevitably affected Tynesiders too. The numbers of unemployed grew and there was little growth for a number of years. However, Newcastle's response to the recession has been amazingly resilient according to the 2012 report from the North-East Economic Forum's (NEEF) annual conference. The regeneration and redevelopment which began at the start of the Millennium has continued despite all odds, attracting new investment and talent which places the region in a much stronger position for economic recovery now than in previous recessions. Strong public-private partnerships in the North-East continue to create the conditions for growth which are crucial to attracting and retaining investment.

Before the recession hit, Newcastle's economy was growing stronger and there is still evidence of market confidence and investment despite the current global economic slowdown, with private sector investment, major city retail extensions already pre-let and new office take-ups across the city centre which open up new jobs and new opportunities. Regeneration challenges are being addressed in the former coalfield areas and in localised areas of high deprivation, particularly with housing developments and refurbishments. Skills' shortages in the workforce are also being tackled with better educational facilities for basic and higher level skills. As the NEEF report commented:

> '. . . The North East is in the unique position of having all the assets required for economic growth on its doorstep and access to everything else it requires through its extensive business networks, academic institutions, transport and

communications infrastructure. The economic prospects for the North East look promising.'

A switched-on city

Indeed, Tyneside's reputation as a centre where dynamic city life meets the three Cs of culture, countryside and coastline has ensured that Newcastle is fast becoming one of the most visited regional capitals in Britain and the city continues to adapt accordingly as we proceed further into the second decade of the noughties. The versatility of the region means that within fifteen minutes of the city centre you can find yourself at the invigorating North Sea coast, or enjoying the peace and tranquillity of the glorious Northumberland countryside. Geordies, visitors and students alike all throng to our friendly, lively city.

Tyneside greeted the advent of the new Millennium with an extravaganza of fireworks, bonfires and non-stop partying. In the year 2000, Newcastle was voted the eighth most popular 'party city' in the world, although quite how that decision was arrived at is still unclear. Many Geordies, disgruntled at this 'low' ranking, strive tirelessly to attain what they see as Newcastle's rightful position as the 'rave capital' of the world. Totally regardless of the weather, swarms of Tyneside's lightly clad lads and lasses pour into the city's numerous pubs in the Bigg Market and Quayside areas each evening. (Remember that 'Bigg' has nothing to do with size – the name actually refers to a particular kind of barley that used to be sold in the market-place long ago!) Newcastle's vibrant nightlife has assumed almost legendary status and revellers from far and wide are drawn to the city's bright lights. Awaiting them is a bewildering number of top class nightclubs, pubs and restaurants, catering for a wide variety of tastes.

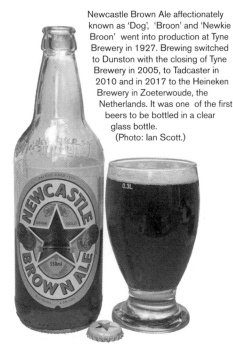

Newcastle Brown Ale affectionately known as 'Dog', 'Broon' and 'Newkie Broon' went into production at Tyne Brewery in 1927. Brewing switched to Dunston with the closing of Tyne Brewery in 2005, to Tadcaster in 2010 and in 2017 to the Heineken Brewery in Zoeterwoude, the Netherlands. It was one of the first beers to be bottled in a clear glass bottle.
(Photo: Ian Scott.)

The city's pubs alone attract thousands of visitors every weekend, and, on football match days, are packed to overflowing. Fine real ales with names like 'Radgie Gadgie' and 'Worky Ticket' rub shoulders with exotic lagers and energy drinks, but pride of place still goes to the one and only Newcastle Brown Ale. Known variously as 'The Dog', 'Broon' and 'Journey into Space',

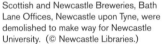

Scottish and Newcastle Breweries, Bath Lane Offices, Newcastle upon Tyne, were demolished to make way for Newcastle University. (© Newcastle Libraries.)

On the site of the old Newcastle Breweries at Gallowgate stands the new Newcastle University Business School. The building was officially opened in March 2012, by Santander UK's Chairman, Lord Burns and the University's Vice-Chancellor, Professor Chris Brink. (Photo: Ian Scott.)

Tyneside's favourite brew was developed in 1927 by Lt Colonel James (Jim) Porter and is one of the UK's best selling bottled beers. It was first brewed at the Tyne Brewery on Corporation Street. Brewing on that site goes back to 1868. The blue star logo was introduced on the label of this brown ale bottle in 1928, the year after its launch, and the five points of the star represent the five founding breweries of Newcastle – not many people know that now! Newcastle Breweries merged with Scottish Brewers in 1960, making Newcastle Brown Ale a flagship brand and giving this beer nationwide distribution, so that by the late nineties it was the most widely distributed alcoholic product in the UK.

The last bottles of 'Broon' came off the production line in Newcastle in April 2005, drawing to a close the 121-year history of brewing at the Tyne Brewery site. Then Scottish & Newcastle moved to Dunston in Gateshead, forming a new company, Newcastle Federation Breweries. The Dunston Brewery closed down in 2010 and brewing moved to John Smith's Brewery in Tadcaster and finally in 2017 to the Heineken Brewery in Zoeterwoude, the Netherlands. This ale is mainly seen as 'a working-man's beer' in the UK and has enjoyed a long association with heavy industry in the North-East. Ironically, it is now viewed as a trendy import around the world and is very popular among the young. Particularly popular on the west coast of America, it is reputed to be a favourite tipple of such superstars as Clint Eastwood and Kevin Costner!

The Tyne Brewery site was bought in 2004 by a consortium of Newcastle City Council, Newcastle University and the then regional development agency One North East (now abolished). Demolition of the old brewery began in March 2007, while the triggering of the controlled demolition of the former Barrack Road bottling plant opposite St James' Park was ceremonially performed by none other than Newcastle's own Sir Bobby Robson on 23 June 2008. The new £50 million Business School of Newcastle University finally emerged from its hoardings on the brewery site in 2011 and was officially opened on 19 March 2012 by Lord Terence Burns. What was formerly the regional office building for Scottish & Newcastle Brewery has now become site of the 175-room, boutique-style Sandman Signature Hotel, which fittingly showcases the famous blue star of Newcastle Brown Ale high atop the exterior of its building, guaranteeing that this iconic logo won't be lost just yet.

Facelifts and farewells

By the year 2000, it had become more and more obvious that something would have to be done about the tower blocks at Cruddas Park, part of T. Dan Smith's Brutalist-architectural modernising plans for Newcastle and a familiar part of the city's skyline since the 1960s. In the intervening years, the area had become the focus of criminal activity and had gained a somewhat notorious reputation. The City Council decided to revamp all ten tower blocks for the twenty-first century, with the aid of private developers. Residents were consulted about making their area a better place to live and plans were drawn up which included new kitchens and bathrooms for flats, new low-rise family homes and a redevelopment of the shopping centre. Work began in the autumn of 2006 and five apartment blocks had undergone a multi-million pound transformation by 2011, making it one of the city's largest housing redevelopment schemes in recent years. The economic problems of the private developers forced the Council's decision to demolish the remaining five empty tower blocks in 2011. This whole area has now been cleaned up and renamed Riverside Dene.

Plans for the continuing refurbishment of the shopping centre now form part of the wider regeneration of the whole of Newcastle's West End, with money made available for landscaping and more local shopping areas. Elswick Park and Elswick Pool have been refurbished to provide better community facilities. New affordable homes have been built in Scotswood at the Rise. A new business and enterprise school, Excelsior Academy, was built in September 2008 to replace

Westgate Community College, and this provides a specialist education for some 1,800 pupils around the area.

In Newcastle's city centre, the years of industrial pollution which blackened the once stunning façades of venerable buildings is now being peeled off in the course of an ongoing programme of restoration. This has considerably brightened up the face of Grainger Town and numerous buildings near and including Central Station, along the Quayside and the lower Ouseburn Valley. Other improvements to the town centre include the very welcome pedestrianisation of Northumberland Street and much of the area around Grey's Monument.

Many of the listed buildings have now been converted into pubs, such as The Union Rooms on Westgate Road, House of Tides restaurant at the Close and various other premises on Grey Street. Although Tyneside's younger, trendier element tends to frequent the modern establishments most geared to its needs, Newcastle still preserves its share of the quieter, more traditional pubs. Three favourites are The Old George Inn, down a cobbled back-alley in Cloth Market, The Bodega, next to the Tyne Theatre and Opera House on Westgate Road, and the excellent Crown Posada, tucked away on the Side and known locally as 'The Coffin' because it is long and narrow, with stained-glass windows and wood-clad walls! However, the city's more sophisticated clientele may be seen in such swish establishments as Barluga on Grey Street and the award-winning, glass-fronted Pitcher and Piano on the Quayside, which boasts fine views of the riverside, BALTIC and the Millennium Bridge.

Along the Quayside itself, nearly a thousand years of history blend together in an intriguing jumble of architectural styles. The area bustles with activity and now features on its promenade a number of fascinating public works of art that reflect Tyneside's heritage across the ages. Prominent amongst these are 'The Blacksmith's Needle', by Alan Dawson, which is a 7.6-metre, conical steel

Car ferry TSS *Caledonian Princess* became the floating nightclub *Tuxedo Princess*, locally known as 'The Boat'. It closed in December 2007 and slipped moorings from under the Tyne Bridge in July 2008. (Photo: Keith Durham.)

The Gateshead Hilton overlooking Gateshead Quayside and the Swing Bridge. (Photo: Graeme Peacock.)

sculpture with a maritime theme represented by mermaids, bells and sea creatures; the 'Swirl Pavilion Sculpture', a two-metre diameter ball by Raf Fulcher, covered in gold leaf and contained within a steel frame surmounting a stone pavilion with the names of various towns carved around its inner rim, located at East Quayside; André Wallace's 'River God' and the 'Siren' are remarkable companion pieces, while Neil Talbot's wonderful 'Relief Sculpture' depicts well-known landmarks along the River Tyne's journey to the sea, all carved into a sandstone wall. But without doubt, the most striking modern work of art to grace Tyneside's riverscape is the magnificent Millennium Bridge, which actually belongs to Gateshead as we have mentioned. A number of hotels of international renown, such as Jury's Inn and the Hilton, have also been built around the Quayside, in addition to many new restaurants and pubs.

When speaking of the Quayside, mention must be made of the history of Newcastle's very own floating nightclub! Buying a second-hand ship to serve as a floating bar and nightclub to be moored on the bank of the River Tyne was the brainwave of Tyneside-based businessman, Michael Quadrini, who already ran the popular Tuxedo Junction nightclub in Newcastle from the 1980s onwards. The *Tuxedo Princess* (formerly TSS *Caledonian Princess*) was a former car ferry which served as a permanently moored, floating nightclub alongside the Swing Bridge from the 1980s into the noughties. She became a Tyneside icon during her stay in Newcastle and was affectionately known as 'The Boat' by Geordies. Many celebrities partied on the *Princess* in her time on Tyneside, including composer Andrew Lloyd Webber, actor Kevin Costner, singers Mick Hucknall and Jason Donovan, pop group 'Frankie Goes to Hollywood', cricketer Ian Botham, snooker player Steve Davis and footballers Kevin Keegan and Paul Gascoigne. In December 2007, a farewell party was held aboard the *Tuxedo Princess* and she was finally towed away from her moorings on 27 July 2008, with crowds of Geordies nostalgically bidding farewell to the end of that era on Tyneside.

Meanwhile, regeneration plans are continually afoot in other run-down

Above: Completed in 2009 as a residential and office block, 15-storey Forth Banks Tower on Forth Banks, commands stunning views down the Tyne. (Photo: Graeme Peacock.)

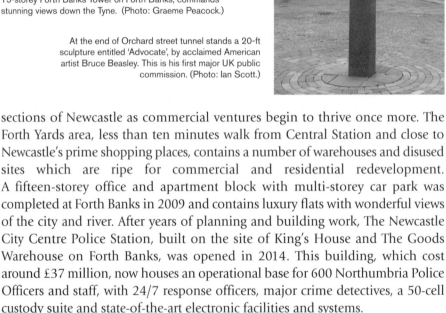

At the end of Orchard street tunnel stands a 20-ft sculpture entitled 'Advocate', by acclaimed American artist Bruce Beasley. This is his first major UK public commission. (Photo: Ian Scott.)

sections of Newcastle as commercial ventures begin to thrive once more. The Forth Yards area, less than ten minutes walk from Central Station and close to Newcastle's prime shopping places, contains a number of warehouses and disused sites which are ripe for commercial and residential redevelopment. A fifteen-storey office and apartment block with multi-storey car park was completed at Forth Banks in 2009 and contains luxury flats with wonderful views of the city and river. After years of planning and building work, The Newcastle City Centre Police Station, built on the site of King's House and The Goods Warehouse on Forth Banks, was opened in 2014. This building, which cost around £37 million, now houses an operational base for 600 Northumbria Police Officers and staff, with 24/7 response officers, major crime detectives, a 50-cell custody suite and state-of-the-art electronic facilities and systems.

At the end of Orchard Street tunnel and within walking distance of Newcastle Central Station stands 'Advocate', a 20-ft tall public artwork in front of Central Square, executed by acclaimed American artist, Bruce Beasley. In June 2014, this permanent artwork replaced the temporary 9-meter high, double-helix of shopping trolleys entitled 'DNA D1.90' by British sculptor Abigail Fallis. Commenting on 'Advocate', Bruce Beasley said: 'I take on shapes like musicians take on notes. Individual notes don't mean anything but when you start putting them together, you get music. A sculpture is like that. I play with shapes until something starts to happen.

Also close by the Central Station is the International Centre for Life, symbol of Newcastle University's ground-breaking research in the field of genetics. Built on what was once a Roman settlement, a hospital and a livestock market, this £60-million Millennium project has completely transformed a run-down area of inner Newcastle. Giving work to almost 600 people, it combines a new block for the University's Genetics department, a Bioscience Centre, with office and laboratory space for private sector bio-technology companies, a wonderful visitor attraction designed to inform the public, both young and old, about genetics and the story of DNA, together with a hotel and multi-storey car park. All of this is contained in Times Square, the first new public square in Newcastle for over a century, which also houses several entertainment venues and bars, as well as space for outdoor events, including an ice rink for the winter months. The Centre for Life was opened by Her Majesty the Queen in 2000, a fitting project for the start of the twenty-first century and its patron is Dr James Watson, the renowned scientist, Nobel Prize winner and co-discoverer in 1953 of the structure of DNA.

Keeping pace with the Centre for Life are the city's hospitals, with closures of old facilities giving way to new developments. Newcastle General Hospital on Westgate Road, which was originally opened as the infirmary for the Newcastle Union Workhouse in 1870 and later became the main hospital for the city, was closed on 16 November 2010, when the Newcastle-upon-Tyne Hospitals NHS Foundation Trust reorganised its provision for acute and tertiary health care. Most of its services were moved to the Royal Victoria Infirmary (RVI) and the Freeman Hospital and its land has been made available for commercial development. The

Opened in 2010, the New Victoria Wing of the RVI includes a state-of-the-art Accident and Emergency department and the Great North Children's Hospital. (Photo: Ian Scott.)

New Victoria Wing of the RVI now includes a state-of-the-art Accident and Emergency department opened in 2010 and the wonderful Great North Children's Hospital. Both the RVI and the Freeman offer excellent health services for all those who live in the North-East.

Infrastructural improvements

To the north of the city centre, Haymarket now functions as a public transport hub, having Eldon Square bus station, Haymarket bus station and Haymarket Metro station all located next to each other and immediately accessible for commuters to and from the city. Haymarket Metro station has been completely rebuilt, at a cost of £20 million, and, under the new title Haymarket Hub, now includes many modern, well-frequented retail outlets. It was officially reopened by the Princess Royal in 2010.

Sadly, Ray Smith's much publicised artwork here is now no more. It had been commissioned in 1999 by the City Council at a cost of £270,000 and Geordies will remember that it stood near to the hexagonal Boer War memorial obelisk with its bronze statue of Nike as Winged Victory, acting as a barrier between the pedestrianised area around the metro station and that very busy road junction. The artwork, consisting of 52 men standing shoulder-to-shoulder, was entitled 'Shoulder to Shoulder' but was known affectionately by Tynesiders as 'The Lego

Men'. It sported a playful water feature which occasionally gave unsuspecting pedestrians an unwelcome soaking in squally weather and this may have been instrumental in the removal of all 52 figures in 2008 at a further cost to the public purse of £70,000. The figures were stored for some years on wasteland near the city centre but some have since been auctioned off by the the City Council on eBay, no less! Indeed, you may be one of the lucky Tynesiders now boasting a Lego Man water feature in your garden or allotment.

A huge increase in traffic using Tyneside's bridges led to an urgent need in the noughties for

Installed in 1999 at a cost around £270,000, 'Shoulder To Shoulder' consisted of 52 concrete figures that were designed to act as a safety barrier to protect pedestrians from heavy traffic around the Boer War Memorial and Haymarket Metro station. The statues quickly became known as 'The Lego Men'. Removed in 2008, they were auctioned on eBay and one is reputed to have been sold for £1,254! (Photo: Ian Scott.)

a second, two-lane, vehicular toll tunnel connecting the town of Jarrow on the south bank of the river with North Shields and Howdon on the north bank. In March 2004, the Tyne and Wear Integrated Transport Authority decided to build a second tunnel, costing £139 million. This second tunnel is slightly to the east of the existing one and the pairing allows each tunnel to serve two lanes of traffic, each travelling in the same direction, whereas the original tunnel completed in 1967 had only two lanes of traffic travelling in opposing directions. Construction work began in the spring of 2008 and the new tunnel opened to two-lane, bi-directional traffic on 25 February 2011. In addition, a £4.9 million refurbishment scheme of the Tyne Pedestrian and Cycle Tunnel was approved in 2012, which included the replacement of two of the original four escalators with lifts, and the replacement of the original tunnel's ageing mechanical and electrical systems. New lighting, CCTV and control and communications systems were also installed. Other repairs were to the tunnel structure itself and to the tiling and panelling. The concrete sections have also been refurbished or replaced, all of which greatly improve the surfaces for cyclists and pedestrians. After a series of delays, the work should be completed in 2018.

The city's airport, once the modest Woolsington Aerodrome, opened in 1935 at a cost of £35,000 and incorporating a small clubhouse, hangar, workshops, fuel garage and grass runway, has over time been completely transformed into Newcastle International Airport, reported as the eleventh busiest airport in the UK in 2012. A new £27-million extension was opened in 2000 and August 2004 saw an extended and refurbished departure terminal opened, with 1,200 new waiting seats, new shops and cafés. A record 5.4 million passengers used Newcastle's airport in 2006! Further developments are planned for the south side of the airport, including maintenance facilities, a new hangar and apron areas,

The new Newcastle International departure terminal. (Photo: Graeme Peacock.)

while there are proposals to improve the capacity of the runway, extend the terminal and upgrade the infrastructure. All of these guarantee that Newcastle will maintain its position as the third largest airport in the North of England, after Manchester and Liverpool, and who knows – it might even outpace these two in the next few decades?

Economic prosperity

In 2002, the ever-adapting city welcomed a new development on Newgate Street to replace the seven-storey Newgate House. The Gate is a three-storey complex of glass and steel, housing numerous bars, restaurants, a casino and a multi-screen cinema. Located behind The Gate is Stowell Street, home to Newcastle's Chinatown. Here, amongst Chinese supermarkets and craft shops, a wide selection of restaurants offers some of the best Asian cuisine on Tyneside, while the city's other restaurants also enjoy a well-deserved reputation for serving a superb range of traditional and ethnic dishes from around the world.

True to form, Newcastle's regeneration continues apace with even more ambitious plans being realised. In June 2005, reconstruction work on Eldon Square began to convert the former bus station into a new lower mall, housing the anchor tenants Argos and Waitrose. The new Eldon Square bus station, which opened on 18 March 2007, between John Lewis department store and the

Replacing the Mayfair Ballroom, The Gate leisure complex is home to many bars, restaurants, a casino and a multiplex cinema. (Photo: Keith Durham.)

A new mall, Eldon Square South was added to the Eldon Square shopping complex, February 2010. (Photo: Ian Scott.)

Haymarket bus station, houses an interesting series of glass screens designed by Newcastle artist Dan Savage. The former Green Market was closed and demolished, but the market shops and wet fish shop were preserved and relocated to the nearby Grainger Market.

This made way for Eldon Square South, a new mall with an enormous Debenham's Department Store as anchor tenant and many other new tenants, including a very welcome Apple Store. Above the shopping malls is a new leisure centre called Eldon Leisure, featuring fitness studios, squash courts and a large sports hall. Eldon Square South opened on 16 February 2010, making the newly-extended, £170-million redevelopment into the largest city centre shopping complex in the UK once again, boasting over 151 stores. The complex has even been rebranded with the new title 'intu Eldon Square'. The refurbishment of various areas of Eldon Square continues apace and the Northumberland Street entrance was demolished in November 2013, to be replaced by a grand new entrance early in 2014. Some £25 million has been spent on the creation of a new dining quarter. This has involved refurbishing the original Sidgate and High Friars malls and reconfiguring 80,000 square feet of retail space in the shopping centre into new restaurant units, opened to the public in 2015.

Educational developments

The areas around Haymarket on the northern edge of the city centre have also seen other new building developments, one of the most prominent being the new King's Gate building, a £22-million, gateway building undertaken by the Sheffield-based practice of Bond Bryan for Newcastle University. This 8,000 square-metre building, opposite St Thomas's Green, provides a modern, airy, five-storey, new 'front door' to the University, housing student support services, all major estates and management administration departments, meeting rooms and social areas. The Duke of York, whose daughter Eugenie was a student at the University, officially opened the King's Gate building on Thursday, 4 February 2010. Newcastle University is now one of the UK's leading international

Newcastle University's King's Gate building on Barras Bridge was opened in 2010 by The Duke of York, whose daughter Princess Eugenie attended as a student. (Photo: Ian Scott.)

University of Northumbria's Campus East and Campus West straddle the Central Motorway and were in need of a link. A new bridge opened by Lord Digby Jones now connects the two campuses. (Photo: Ian Scott.)

universities in the fields of medicine and science and we have already mentioned its state-of-the-art Genetics Department located at The Centre for Life near Central Station.

Not to be outdone, Newcastle's second university has also seen major building developments and was voted 'Best New University' by *The Times Good University Guide 2005*. Northumbria's city campus is now divided into City Campus East and City Campus West by the city's central motorway and linked by a new, £4-million bridge, officially opened in 2006 by Lord Digby Jones. City Campus East, opened in September 2007, houses the Schools of Law, Design, Fashion and Marketing and the Newcastle Business School, and has become an architectural landmark in the city. Designed by Atkins, it has won numerous awards and accolades for its excellence as a building project. City Campus West houses the Schools of Arts and Social Sciences, Computing, Engineering and Sciences and the university library amongst others, including a £30-million central sports facility opened in 2010 for students, staff and the community.

Culture vultures

Some of the greatest success stories in Newcastle of the noughties lie in the area of culture. The Great North Museum Project is a £26-million refurbishment and extension of the Hancock Museum in Newcastle by architects Terry Farrell and Partners. This ambitious project has brought together and ensured the permanent survival of its natural history and art collections alongside archaeological artefacts and interactive exhibits. It features three venues: The Great North Museum: Hancock, which now also includes the collections of the Newcastle University's Museum of Antiquities and the Shefton Museum of Greek art and archaeology; The Hatton Gallery in the Fine Art building on Newcastle's University campus, and the Regional Resource Centre located in the basement of the Discovery Museum in Blandford Square. The project received generous funding from many quarters, including the Heritage Lottery Fund and countless individual donors, and was officially opened on 6 November 2009 by Her Majesty the Queen, receiving over 600,000 visitors in the first few months alone.

The Great North Museum Library is also open to the public. Located on the second floor of the Hancock, it houses three important collections: the Natural History Society of Northumbria's library and archives, the Society of Antiquaries of Newcastle upon Tyne's library and Newcastle University's Cowen Library. As well as now incorporating the collections of the Shefton Museum and the Museum of Antiquities, Hancock's Natural History Museum is packed with interesting objects, including an interactive model of Hadrian's Wall, an interactive Bio-Wall, a full size model of an elephant, a great white shark display and a moa skeleton. While across the road the Hatton Gallery, located in the University's Fine Art Building, features an eclectic collection comprising over 3,500 paintings, sculptures, prints and drawings, including the Merzbarn Wall – the only surviving Merz construction by world-famous artist Kurt Schwitters.

Closely connected to the Great North Museum Project is the Discovery Museum, a science and local history museum located in Blandford Square. It started life as the Municipal Museum of Science and Industry, housed in a temporary pavilion at Exhibition Park in Newcastle and had the distinction then of being the first UK science museum outside London. In 1978, the collections had grown to such an extent that the museum was relocated to Blandford House, the former Co-operative Wholesale Society Headquarters for the Northern Region, which had a lot more room. This magnificent 1899 building, designed by Oliver, Leeson and Wood, had been the distribution centre for over 100 Co-op stores across the region and contained extensive warehouse and office space. In 1993, the Museum was re-launched as the award-winning Discovery Museum, with many spectacular displays of local history, including *Turbinia*, the 34-metre long ship built by Charles Algernon Parsons to test the advantages of using the steam turbine to power ships, which resides in majestic splendour in the entrance hall. Ongoing refurbishments have brought many new displays and more than half a million visitors enter its portals each year.

Newcastle's Literary & Philosophical Society on Westgate Road, that 'conversation club' which has flourished since its foundation in 1793, is now the largest independent library outside of London, containing over 150,000 books covering every field of interest, both fiction and non-fiction. Its music library is unequalled in the North of England, containing over 8,000 CDs and 10,000 LPs. Still located in its original building, it has free reference facilities as well as lending facilities for members. In February 2011, Alexander Armstrong, the Rothbury-born actor, comedian and presenter of the popular TV quiz show *Pointless*, became President of the Lit & Phil. He launched their funding appeal at a special gala event and this proved a powerful incentive in the revival of the Society's membership, so that at the beginning of 2012, the number of members reached 2,000, its highest since 1952.

To the delight of all Tynesider bookworms, Newcastle's new City Library was officially opened on 6 November 2009 by the Queen and Duke of Edinburgh, on a site which has housed a free lending library since Victorian times. The old Victorian building

The 'hands-on' Discovery Museum in Blandford Square is designed to interest all ages. The museum displays many exhibits of local history, including Sir Charles Parson's *Turbinia* and examples of Joseph Swan's early lightbulbs. It houses the regimental museum for the 15th/19th The King's Royal Hussars and the Northumberland Hussars. In 2006 it was winner of the North-East's Best Family Experience award at the North-East England Tourism Awards. (Photo: Graeme Peacock.)

had been demolished in the 1960s to make way for an ugly Brutalist construction colourfully described by local TV presenter and author John Grundy as 'a monstrous concrete blob'. Thankfully, this was demolished in 2007 and the foundation stone marking the new library's construction was laid by the Lord Mayor on 17 December 2007. The new City Library is called the Charles Avison Building in honour of the famous, eighteenth-century Newcastle composer and musician. Its six storeys contain a marble-floored atrium, a 185-seater performance space for lectures, concerts and entertainment, a 100-seater café, an exhibition area, a fully-equipped crèche, meeting rooms and free internet facilities, plus all the modern technologies of libraries nowadays, including online catalogues, digital tags on books, and automated checkout points.

The new Newcastle City Library (Charles Avison Building) was opened in 2009 by the Queen and Duke of Edinburgh. It replaced the 1960s building, described as 'a monstrous blob' by John Grundy. (Photo: Graeme Peacock.)

The neighbouring Laing Art Gallery on New Bridge Street boasts an outstanding collection of watercolours and oils, including some Pre-Raphaelite masterpieces, prints, drawings, sculpture and decorative arts, which have been steadily built up over the years through purchases and donations from local collectors, including Heritage Lottery funding. All the major genres within Victorian art are represented, together with an excellent collection by locally-born British Romantic artist John Martin, whose work also features in Tate Britain and international galleries. Twentieth-century artists represented include John Singer Sargent, Augustus John, John Lavery, William Orpen, Walter Sickert and Stanley Spencer. In addition, there are excellent collection of Newcastle silverware, enamelled glassware by William Beilby and North-East ceramics, including Maling pottery. Although predominantly British in character, there is also a small but important collection of European paintings. Indeed, over the past hundred years, the Laing has been transformed from the almost empty building which first opened its doors in 1904 into the North-East's premier art gallery.

The open space in front of the Laing Art Gallery houses an unusual square called 'The Blue Carpet'. Designed by Thomas Heatherwick and completed in

2001, this square has been covered in what resembles a carpet of blue paving slabs, produced by mixing crushed blue glass with resin. A number of benches stand on the surface of this 'carpet' and beneath the benches are sunken, glass-topped boxes which house coloured lights. At the eastern end a new staircase featuring a curving skin of wood ribbons leads to an elevated walkway. This development, together with the new City Library, has greatly improved the streetscape of this area, although it has now become the subject of local debate because parts of it are used as ramps by skateboarders, and the blue tiles have also faded to a blue-grey colour which was not envisaged in the original Heatherwick design.

A special mention must be made here of the lower Ouseburn Valley, which has now become a cultural and social oasis, close to the city centre. The Ouseburn, a small tributary of the mighty River Tyne, once played an important role in Newcastle's industrial revolution as we have seen, when coal was brought from the Town Moor along the Victoria Tunnel, where the tidal nature of the Ouseburn allowed keels to be loaded at low tide and pulled out to the collier brigs waiting on the Tyne River. However, by the end of the nineteenth century, the lower part of the Ouseburn Valley had fallen into disuse, and its many large warehouses and mills, the relics of its industrial heyday, lay derelict. From 1996 onwards, the Ouseburn Development Trust, in partnership with the local authority, has led this area's regeneration as a cultural mecca and has been so successful that the lower Ouseburn Valley is now marketed as a very trendy place to live. The Valley is also home to a number of pubs, known locally for live music, real ale and good food, well worth exploring on a sunny afternoon.

The Victoria Tunnel runs under Newcastle from the Town Moor down to the River Tyne. Built between 1839-42 to transport coal from Leazes Main Colliery in Spital Tongues to the riverside staithes to be loaded onto ships. (Photo: courtesy Ouseburn Trust.)

One of the finest examples of industrial architecture on the Lower Ouseburn is a seven-storey warehouse on Lime Street, dating from the 1870s and originally used by Messrs Procter and Sons to store grain and flour for an adjoining flour mill. In 2005, it was fully renovated and reopened as Seven Stories, a huge national centre dedicated to children's literature and spanning the full seven floors of the warehouse and mill. Tynesiders can be very proud of this as it is the only place in the UK dedicated to the art of children's books and one of just a few such places in the world. Inside Seven Stories there are display exhibitions exploring every aspect of children'

Right: The Biscuit Factory in Shieldfield is a commercial art gallery and home to two floors of exhibitions, plus studios and cafés.
(Photo: Graeme Peacock.)

Below: Seven Stories, as the name suggests, is on seven floors and it is the only place in the UK dedicated to the art of children's books.
(Photo: courtesy Seven Stories.)

literature. Showcased here is a huge collection of unique manuscripts, artwork, illustrations and other documents from authors such as Michael Rosen, Nina Bawden, Phillip Pullman, David Almond, Kaye Webb, Judith Kerr, Enid Blyton and over 100 other children's authors and book illustrators. The centre is very child-orientated and designed to create a lifetime's love of reading. Here children can enjoy workshops, meet-the-writer sessions, the Storyboat, the multi-media story lab, the Seven Stories theatre and other special events associated with the magic world of storytelling.

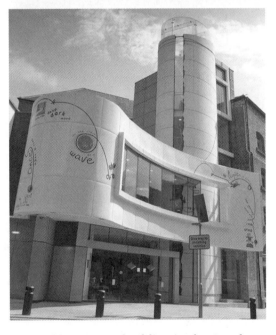

The Biscuit Factory is housed in an old Victorian building in the Ouseburn Valley which used to manufacture biscuits. The name of this building has changed over the years from 'The Tyne Biscuit Factory' to 'Newcastle upon Tyne Biscuit Manufacturers' and the factory was also used as a carpet and furniture warehouse before undergoing major renovation work in 2001 to become a commercial art gallery, while still retaining its name. The building consists of two floors of exhibition space and two floors of artists' studios, with a café and restaurant. Gallery spaces display a range of contemporary fine art, sculpture, original prints, jewellery and design-led homeware. Four major exhibitions are hosted here each year, changing on a quarterly basis and representing the work of about 250 artists during each season. It is well worth a visit for art lovers and browsers alike.

Another iconic building located at the mouth of the Ouseburn is The Toffee

The Toffee Factory, once Maynards toffee factory in Lower Ouseburn, has now been turned into office space, targeting graphic designers, software engineers and architects. (Photo: Graeme Peacock.)

Factory in the Lower Steenbergs Yard. Built in 1878 by Newcastle Corporation as an extension to the sanatorium used for quarantining foreign cattle imports, it was never used as such. Eventually leased by John Vose in 1895, it became a toffee factory. Vose later sold his successful business to Maynards Sweet Company. who leased the factory in 1906. Apart from Maynards' Toffees, Geordies of a certain age will remember savouring Acid Drops, Black Bullets, Brazils, Pear Drops, and Humbugs. The factory ceased production in the late 1950s and Steenbergs company leased the empty premises for storage in the 1980s but moved out after a few years. In 1993, the factory was severely damaged by fire. Its sad shell stood roofless and derelict until its transformation into The Toffee Factory in late 2011, led by Xsite Architecture, an Ouseburn-based firm. The refurbished Victorian building has scooped a number of architectural and design awards and been highly commended in the North East RICS awards. It is now home to over twenty creative and digital businesses, employing over 150 staff.

Geordies at play and rest

The Newcastle Falcons rugby union goes from strength to strength and is currently the only professional rugby club in the North-East with one Premiership and four domestic cups to its name. Many home-grown rugby stalwarts swell the team's ranks, and what Geordie's voice wasn't hoarse with cheers watching Jonny Wilkinson score that magnificent, winning drop goal in the last minute of extra time against Australia in the 2003 Rugby World Cup final? Jonny, acknowledged as one of the world's best rugby union players, was well-known at Kingston Park, having already played twelve seasons (1997-2009) in the English Premiership with the Newcastle Falcons. The capacity of the Falcons' Kingston Park stadium has been increased in the noughties to keep pace with the increasing numbers now following rugby union on Tyneside. The stadium, bought by Northumbria

University in late 2008 and leased back to Newcastle Falcons, now has a capacity of 10,200 people, with the West Stand being the newest and most modern. There are also plans to expand the North Stand to provide even more facilities for the fans.

Meanwhile back in Gallowgate, St James' Park, the oldest and largest football stadium in the North-East and one of the largest in England, still dominates the horizon and remains the spiritual home of thousands of Newcastle United supporters. Between 1998 and 2000, double tiers were added to the Milburn and John Hall stands to bring the venue up to its current capacity of 52,405 people. This stadium was used as a football venue for the 2012 Olympics, for the 2015 Rugby World Cup and for the 2015, 2016, 2017 and 2018 Super League Magic Weekend. It has also hosted charity events and rock concerts.

The ever popular Bobby Robson took over as manager of Newcastle United from 1999 to 2004 and, by the end of the 2002 season, had steered the club into the top end of the Champions' League, leading the club to the UEFA Cup semi-final in 2004. He received a knighthood in 2002 for his services to the game and was given the freedom of the city in March 2005. Sadly, Sir Bobby died of cancer in July 2009, aged just 76. To commemorate him, a three-metre bronze statue by local sculptor Tom Maley now stands outside the south-west corner of the stadium. A memorial garden, dedicated to his memory, was commissioned by Newcastle City Council and opened in the presence of scores of fans on 22 May 2011. The garden is situated on the former Carnegie Electric site in the shadow of St James' Park, and has five carved stones, each one representing an era of the much-loved Sir Bobby's career. Since Sir Bobby's time, managers have come and gone and Newcastle United's fortunes wax and wane, continuing to excite and disappoint the club's fans in turn. However, one thing is certain, the city will continue to reverberate with the deafening roar of Newcastle United's ever-loyal 'Toon Army'.

Commissioned by Newcastle City Council, the memorial garden to Sir Bobby Robson was opened in May 2011 in front of scores of fans. The five carved stones each represent an era of his career. (Photo: Ian Scott.)

18
GATESHEAD IN THE NOUGHTIES

Gateshead can never be accused of sleeping on the job in this age of progress. Its Millennium Bridge set the pace, closely followed by the Sage Music Centre and the BALTIC Centre for Contemporary Art. Further developments continue into the noughties, concentrating now on improvements in the town centre and the educational needs of the community,

Retail revival

Gateshead's market square, dominated for many years by a deteriorating, multi-storey car park, a forlorn, untenanted, rooftop café and an unattractive shopping precinct on two levels with very poor access, has now been completely transformed. In 2008, Tesco plc acquired an interest in the Trinity Square site, and by working with its subsidiary division Spenhill Development, and the go-ahead Gateshead Council, they have together brought about the complete regeneration of what was up until recently a drab and dismal town centre.

Trinity Square is an exciting, £1-billion complex, designed by Edinburgh architects 3D Reid, and located right in the heart of the town opposite the Gateshead Interchange. It is a major mixed-use development, reconnecting the surrounding, more traditional, streets of Gateshead through a series of pedestrianised routes across the newly-developed site, and has a brand new Town Square at its centre. The largest project of its kind outside London, it offers a Tesco Extra store, around forty new shops, bars and restaurants, a twelve-screen cinema and a Primary Care Centre. In addition, eight blocks of varying mass and height on a high-level podium form the location of a 993-bed student residence complex for Northumbria University. Trinity Square has attracted modern high street retailers and leisure operators and employs over 1,000 people - a huge bonus for Tynesiders of all ages.

Initially, the decision to demolish the iconic *Get Carter* Carpark landmark was unpopular. Once the the Trinity Square site was levelled in October 2010, a huge tower crane was moved in and dominated the skyline for almost a year. At a height of 266 feet, this tower crane was reckoned to be tall enough to place two statues of the 'Angel of the North' in position on top of each other and then mount them on top of Gateshead's BALTIC Centre for Contemporary Art! The crane was immediately put to work lifting and positioning the many thousands of tonnes of steel and other building materials, as the new complex took shape.

When its job was finished, another, even larger, crane was brought in to dismantle it. This 330-feet, 500-tonne, travelling crane was brought all the way from Scotland to dismantle the tower crane on site, and the removal of the 214-foot-long main jib was a spectacular feat for all those who witnessed it with bated breath, not least the crane operators.

More than 1,500 people called the Tesco's recruitment hotline on its first day, all keen to apply for the 200 new jobs in the new Tesco Extra store. The store now employs around 500 people in total, including the 250 employees from the town's original Gateshead Tesco, and the regeneration partnership between Tesco and the town council contains a pledge that 30% of the new staff should be

Local artist Steve Newby's stainless steel sculpture 'Halo' in Gateshead's Trinity Square is the largest of its kind in the world. The eye-catching 'Halo' is made up of 330 separate sections, moulded using a pioneering technique called 'inflating', patented by Steve and stretches 27 feet across. Illuminated at night by interior fibre-optic lights, this sculpture is a 'modern nod' to the town's steel industry traditions and its ring shape symbolises the area's regeneration.
(Photo: courtesy of Trinity Square, Gateshead.)

Viewed from the north, the Trinity Square complex dominates the Gateshead skyline.
(Photo: Ian Scott.)

chosen from the long-term unemployed of the area.

Not to be outdone by this venture, Capital Shopping Centres, owner of the Gateshead Metro Centre, Newcastle's Eldon Square shopping centre and ten other shopping centres throughout the country, has created a national brand for all its centres. These have been rebranded with the prefix 'intu', thus Gateshead Metro Centre is now called 'intu Metrocentre', and Eldon Square is now 'intu Eldon Square'. It's hard to keep up with all the changing names but the overall aim is to encourage more shoppers to spend longer and longer in these mega malls.

At present, intu Metrocentre is ranked second in the UK for overall attractiveness. At 1.9 million square feet and with around 330 shops and department stores, a cinema and bowling alley, it remains Europe's largest covered shopping and leisure centre to date. Together with the adjacent Metro Retail Park, this is now marketed as a 'complete retail, catering and leisure experience', so Tynesiders and visitors to the area should find this a shoppers' paradise!

Educational innovations

In the field of education, Gateshead has forged ahead too. While Newcastle has its two universities, Gateshead has its own progressive facilities for further education as well, focusing on the delivery of vocational and academic courses. Gateshead College, originally established in November 1955 at Durham Road in Low Fell, moved in January 2008 to a new £39-million main site located in the centre of the Baltic Business Quarter on Gateshead Quays. The firm of architects who designed this impressive state-of-the-art campus was the Red Box Design Group. A broad range of facilities are provided on campus: a gym and aerobics studio, salon and spa, art and design studios, ICT suite, learning resource centre and a 200-seater performance theatre, coupled with sound-proofed music rehearsal and recording studios, and there is even a Japanese garden.

The college focuses on further education for 16-18 year olds, specialising in apprenticeships and vocational training, part-time adult learning and training courses for employers, as well as some academic areas. Its campuses now stretch across six sites, from Gateshead Quays, through the Team Valley to Washington in Sunderland and it has seen the investment of more than £75 million in their development. The Team Valley site houses an AutoSkills Centre and two Skills Academies: Construction (in the former Rolls Royce headquarters), and Automotive, Engineering, Manufacturing & Logistics, while the Washington site houses the Skills Academy for Sustainable Manufacturing & Innovation. There is also an Academy for Sport for sports students, based appropriately at Gateshead International Stadium, with an 83m-long athletic hall, an aerobics centre, a

Gateshead College's new £39-million main site located in the centre of the Baltic Business Quarter on Gateshead Quays. (Photo: Ian Scott).

performance lab, outdoor artificial and grass pitches and a floodlit throwing area. It's no wonder that prestigious sports academies and élite athletes train here, alongside the College's own sports students.

Gateshead College is top of the league as regards awards and commendations and is the preferred training provider for Nissan UK Ltd. The winner of two National Training Awards, it has been named the best college for apprenticeships in the North-East region, the most successful Train-to-Gain provider and an educational Centre for Excellence, as well as winning other awards too numerous to mention.

In December 2011, the College established the company Zero Carbon Futures, to deliver a range of local and national programmes to advance the North-East as a European leader in the production of low-carbon vehicles. The company is based in the College's new £10-million Skills Academy for Sustainable Manufacturing and Innovation in Washington, which has a performance test track and vehicle development workshop for testing and trialling new transport technologies. Thus, Gateshead College is also a market leader in the development of low-carbon vehicle technologies and encouraging its students to do their bit for the survival of the planet.

The Quayside Games

The Great North City Games is a wonderful sporting event which has become an established highlight on the summer athletics calendar, when some of the finest international athletes from both sides of the Atlantic get together to test their prowess on the Newcastle-Gateshead Quayside on the day before the Bupa Great North Run. Now in its sixth year, these Games bring world-class competitors to the Quayside and the councils on both sides of the Tyne work together to make it a wonderful day for olympians, paralympians and spectators alike.

These unique City Games get better each year and provide a real appetiser for the Great North Run on the following day. Top athletes from Great Britain and Northern Ireland take on their rivals from the USA and elsewhere on a purpose-built track in the heart of the city. The running-track is created in an iconic setting in front of Sage Gateshead, set against the spectacular backdrop of the Gateshead Millennium Bridge and the other Tyne bridges. Because of its location, spectators can get close to where it's all happening. Crowds of nearly 30,000 have watched the performances of world-famous athletes including Mo Farah, Greg Rutherford, James Dasaolu, Christine Ohurougu and Jonnie Peacock of Great Britain, Dawn Harper, Christian Taylor and David Oliver of the USA and Sally Pearson of Australia. The atmosphere is unbelievable and best news of all is that there is no admission charge to get up close and personal with your athletic heroes and heroines – it's all completely free!

The City Games are part of a world-class weekend of sport on the banks of the Tyne. The Junior and Mini Great North Run takes place on the Saturday and the Bupa Great North Run on Sunday. Now the largest half-marathon in the world, over 50,000 competitors take to the streets over a 13.1 mile course from Newcastle, across the iconic Tyne Bridge, through Gateshead and on to the scenic coastal finish in South Shields. When our own Olympic medallist Brendan Foster first organised the Run back in 1981, little did he think that it would grow year on year to become one of the largest running events in the world.

The Great North City Games are held on the Newcastle-Gateshead Quayside on the Saturday and the Bupa Great North Run on the Sunday, making it a fantastic weekend of sport. (Photos: courtesy Nova International.)

WHERE IT ALL BEGAN

When the Romans first harnessed the potential of the mighty Tyne waterway, little did they realise the enormous developments that would take place over the intervening centuries around this river's banks, first creating a settlement, then a town, then a city called Newcastle with Gateshead on the opposite bank, then a region called Tyneside and a people proud to call it their home.

Over the centuries Tyneside has produced a prestigious line of inventors, engineers, architects, industrialists and entrepreneurs, all of whom have transformed the region and influenced the very course of British and world history. However, none of their achievements would have been possible without Tyneside's dynamic, adaptable and industrious population and the ever-constant, flowing Tyne. The established industries and enterprising workforce are ever adapting and diversifying into new markets, now taking their part in a worldwide economy.

As Tyneside passes confidently through the second Millennium, it will doubtless face many more new and exciting challenges and periods of change as far-reaching as any that have gone before. Judging by its people's pas performance and present adaptability, the region will meet these challenges head-on. Fortified by a tradition of resolve and flexibility, Tyneside will continue to prosper and progress, its future secure in the hands of its unique people, the Geordies, who will forever remain 'the Pride of the Tyne'.

The 'River God Tyne' was one of nine masks (eight principal rivers and the ocean) adorning the Strand front of Somerset House in London, when it was rebuilt in 1786. Carved in stone by Carlini to a design by Sir William Chambers, the river Tyne is represented by a bearded head, surmounted by a basket of burning coals, with fish and other emblems of local trades. This photograph shows a representation of the mask on the side of the Northumberland Arms, Northumberland Street. (Photo: Ian Scott)

INDEX